A Guide To Obtaining Veterans Administration Compensation Benefits

Improve your chances of success when filing a claim with the Veterans Administration

By

Charles Fettes
MCPO, USN (retired)

Reduce delays in your
award of benefits and compensation

Dedication

"Shortly after the formation of the Citrus County Veterans Advisory Board (of which I am a member) in October of 2011, our County Service Officer, Charles Fettes, showed us a rough draft of the first eighteen pages of a booklet he had begun to work on to assist local veterans in their attempt to obtain benefits. He explained that he intended to concentrate on only the benefit of compensation, and that he was hoping to receive a few donations from local veterans groups in hopes of printing it. He also planned to offer it in pdf format via another member's website.

We had no idea of how extensive the finished document would turn out to be. Mr. Fettes has written one of the best "how to" guides I have ever come across. He has helped hundreds of local veterans obtain their benefits, and now, after two revisions, 2100 booklets printed and distributed, and over ten thousand downloads, he has decided to release it nationally in hopes of helping thousands more.

I am proud to have been part of the original initiative which allowed for the publication of this fine manual, and I hope that you find it useful in obtaining your lawful benefits."

Carlton J. McLeod
Rear Admiral, DC,, USN (retired)

A portion of the proceeds from sales of this book will be donated to Citrus County, Florida's Operation Welcome Home program and the Citrus County Veterans Foundation.

Edited by Disabled Vietnam Veteran
Chief Master Sergeant Johnny E. Stewart, USAF (retired)

Disclaimer

This publication is provided solely as an aid to better understand the Veterans Administration compensation claim filing process based upon the Author's personal experience and known data at time of publication. You should, however, confirm all statements contained herein with your local Veterans Service Office before taking any action. It is your responsibility to use this information at your own risk. Permission must be obtained from the Author prior to reproduction.

First Edition

Printed in the United States of America

Contents

Contents (continued)

Forward

****

Since 1993 I have been assisting veterans in obtaining their lawful benefits. It has been rewarding work, and I am grateful to be able to help our country's heroes. In truth, I feel a tremendous obligation to assist our veterans in any way possible.

This guide to obtaining compensation is an answer to those veterans who want to know how the process should be carried out. I have tried to give them a complete guideline without making the process seem overly complicated.

This guide should be passed on to someone who will find it helpful, rather than keeping it on a bookshelf. I was assisted by several caring individuals and organizations with the express purpose of allowing our veterans to obtain their benefits. I thank them for their help, and hope those who use the guide will achieve their goals.

Special thanks got to Chief Master Sergeant (retired) Johnny Stewart who edited this book.

Charles Fettes
January 2013

Introduction

The Department of Veteran's Affairs issues millions of dollars in compensation benefits to our nations veterans every month. Unfortunately, many veterans have no idea what they have to do to obtain the benefits they are entitled to by law. This document is intended to serve as a guide for the purpose of obtaining compensation. There are several other benefits available to veterans from the VA which are beyond the scope of this guide. Please refer to *www.va.gov* for the complete list of available benefits.

The Department of Veterans Affairs defines disability compensation as a monetary benefit which is paid to veterans who are disabled by an injury or illness incurred or aggravated during their time on active duty in the U.S. Military. The term used to refer to these disabilities is "service connected". Any individual who served on active duty for one day or more may be eligible for compensation, provided a claimed disability can be related back to service. The federal guidelines and regulations for determination of service connected disability are listed in title 38 of the code of federal regulations. The regulations and guidelines can be viewed online at *http://www.benefits.va.gov/warms/topics.asp*.

The amount of compensation is set up by the degree of disability. The degree of disability is determined mainly by the effect on the veteran's ability to obtain and maintain employment. Benefits begin at ten percent, and continue at twenty, thirty, etc. with the maximum rating of one hundred

B17 Flying Fortress

percent. The number of the veteran's dependents also affects disability payments. Any veteran who is married and /or has minor children or stepchildren will receive additional benefits with a disability rating of thirty percent or more, as long as they live with the veteran or he or she can prove support for these dependents. Under certain conditions, the veteran may claim his or her parents as dependents. Those veterans with extremely severe conditions may be eligible for "Special Monthly

Compensation" which also will increase payments.

The type of discharge given to a veteran can also affect payments. Any veteran who was discharged dishonorably is not eligible for compensation. Incarcerated veterans will have their payments lowered to the ten percent disability rate if imprisoned more than sixty days if rated at twenty percent or more, and half of the ten percent rate if rated at ten percent. Fugitive felons will have their compensation benefits stopped entirely.

Those veterans rated at less than fifty percent who retired from the military will have their retirement

F-86 Sabre

pay offset by the amount of compensation they are receiving. At the fifty percent rating, a program known as concurrent receipt will make up the difference. Concurrent receipt will start automatically upon meeting the fifty percent rate for those in receipt of military retirement.

Not every veteran will be eligible for compensation. The reasons vary, but many simply have no proof that a claimed condition began in the military. Some veterans simply give up when confronted with the frustration and confusion which comes from dealing with a government institution. This guide should help the veteran have a positive outcome when claiming disability benefits, but there are no guarantees of success. Veterans should be prepared for some setbacks when attempting to establish a condition as service connected. No matter the problem, it's important to remember that every decision rendered by the Department of Veterans Affairs is subject to the appellate process. Nothing is final until the Court of Appeals in Washington D.C. declares the case closed. The keys to a successful outcome are diligence and a great deal of patience. Some claims will take years to resolve, and even the quickest take several months.

Current compensation rates of payment including the allowance for dependents can be found online at:

http://www.vba.va.gov/bln/21/Rates/comp01.htm

Please note that VA compensation benefits have no effect on social security payments or vice versa.

Obtaining Assistance in Filing a Claim

As a rule of thumb, nothing associated with filing a claim for disability compensation should cost the veteran anything. There are several means of obtaining help in filing for a claim, all of which are provided free of charge.

Veterans Service Organizations have National and State Service Officers, accredited by the Department of Veterans Affairs which certifies their ability to represent the veteran in VA matters. These organizations are chartered by Congress, and generally work in partnership with the VA to ensure the veteran receives the maximum benefit available. These Organizations include the American legion, Veterans of Foreign Wars, Disabled American Veterans, Military Order of the Purple Heart, Vietnam Veterans of America, the Marine Corps League, Catholic War Veterans, AMVETS, Jewish War Veterans, Non-Commissioned Officers Association, Paralyzed Veterans and the Polish Legion. Other Institutions such as the American Red Cross may also provide assistance in filing claims. Each VA Regional Office has a number of accredited service officers from these organizations working nearby. There are also local post and chapter veterans service officers which will assist in filing for benefits. A simple search of the area phone book should reveal the numbers of the local Veterans Organizations. All services are of no cost to the veteran. Service Officers associated with these groups will request submission of VA Form 21-22 (available at *www.va.gov/vaforms*) which allows them to represent you before the VA and access to your records.

A-10

Many areas have State, County and City service officers to assist local veterans in obtaining benefits free of charge. These individuals are trained in this work by the veterans service organizations and the Department of Veterans Affairs, and many are accredited through the service organizations. A search of the county and city listings in the phone book should provide the locations of these service officers.

The Department of Veterans Affairs itself will provide assistance in filing for benefits. A visit to the local regional office will provide personal assistance in filing out claim forms, or online through the VONAPP (Veterans Online Applications) program at *www.va.gov*. The VA may be contacted nationwide at 1-800-827-1000 at any time. Once again, assistance is free of charge.

There are many non-veteran organizations which will "assist" you in filing for benefits, which require donations or payments. These groups are not accredited, and are ineffective in achieving positive outcomes. Many are doing this work illegally. The question a veteran should always ask is "Are you accredited with the Department of Veterans Affairs?". A visit to *http://www.va.gov/ogc/apps/accreditation/index.asp* will ascertain the validity of their credentials.

Many veterans feel a lawyer is required to successfully obtain benefits. This is, of course, the veteran's prerogative, and many lawyers will provide the service free of charge to the veteran. Some lawyers do charge the veteran for their assistance, and payment is the responsibility of that veteran. Any veteran hiring a lawyer should have a thorough discussion of the fees associated with their assistance.

Getting Started

Prior to filing a claim for compensation benefits, there are certain things that are necessary for a successful outcome. The following pages will have a discussion of each of them, and how they can be accomplished.

Informal Claims

The first step to filing a claim for benefits is to inform the Department of Veterans Affairs of the intention to do so. This is known as an informal claim. An informal claim will

Abbot

preserve an effective date for any grant of benefits for up to a year. In other words, a successful claim filed eleven months after an informal claim is documented will be granted as of the date of the informal claim. This can mean thousands of dollars in compensation benefits to the veteran!

An informal claim can consist of nothing more than a phone call to the VA Nationwide toll free number 1-800-827-1000 and stating the intention to file a claim for benefits. A better option is to file a written notice via VA Form 21-4138 (a general statement form) with the VA, stating the intention to file, and what benefit the veteran is seeking (i.e. compensation for a left knee condition). The 21-4138 can be obtained through a veteran's service officer or online at *http://www.va.gov*/vaforms, as can any other VA form sought. The application can be submitted electronically via the VONAPP program at *www.va.gov* or via mail to the nearest VA Regional Office. The address of the Regional Office in the veteran's area can be found using the locator function at the *www.va.gov* website.

HMMWV

Proof of Service

Any claim with the Department of Veterans Affairs requires documentation of service. No claim can begin unless the veteran can provide proof of active duty service. For most this proof is via a DD 214. The DD 214 identifies the veteran and lists the dates of service, duty stations, overseas service, medals and awards, educational accomplishments, rank, service number (prior to 1970), date and place of birth, character of discharge and whether the veteran received wounds as a result of combat. There is a long form and a short form of the DD 214. The long form is the document that the VA requires. This form specifically cites the character of service (i.e. honorable, general, etc.). Before January 1, 1950, several similar forms were used by the military services, including the WD AGO 53, WD AGO 55, WD AGO 53-55, NAVPERS 553, NAVMC 78PD, and the NAVCG 553.

For most claims, the DD214 alone is not enough. Every service member should have a copy of his or her entire military record. This includes both the medical and personnel records. If not already in their possession, the veteran can obtain these records through the National Personnel Records Center in St. Louis via Standard Form 180. Standard Form 180 can be obtained from any Veterans Service Officer or online at *www.archives.gov/veterans/military-service-records*. The form can be filed electronically or sent via mail to:

National Personnel Records Center
1 Archives Drive
St. Louis, Missouri 63138

When filling out the Standard Form 180, ensure that an undeleted report of separation is requested. This will make certain that the character of discharge is displayed on the document.

Please note that the records repository experienced a major fire in 1973 which led to the loss of thousands of military personnel and medical records. The records repository will attempt to

AMX-40

reconstruct the records if this was the case, but not all attempts will be successful. The veteran may have to rely on other means to document his or her service.

For example, if compensation is requested as a result of a specific incident which may not be documented in personnel or medical records, morning reports, ships logs, roster reports, casualty reports can also be requested for specific time frames via Standard Form 180. In general, this type of request will take longer to fill than the simple requests for personnel and medical records.

Once proof of service and the military records are obtained, it's time for the veteran to gather necessary evidence to support his claim for benefits.

The periods of war associated with VA benefits are as follows:

• World War II. December 7, 1941, through December 31, 1946, inclusive. If the veteran was in service on December 31, 1946, continuous service before July 26, 1947, is considered World War II service.

• Korean conflict, June 27, 1950, through January 31, 1955, inclusive.

- Vietnam era. The period beginning on February 28, 1961, and ending on May 7, 1975, inclusive, in the case of a veteran who served in the Republic of Vietnam during that period. The period beginning on August 5, 1964, and ending on May 7, 1975, inclusive, in all other cases.(Authority: 38 U.S.C. 101(29))
- Future dates. The period beginning on the date of any future declaration of war by the Congress and ending on a date prescribed by Presidential proclamation or concurrent resolution of the Congress.(Authority: 38 U.S.C. 101)
- Persian Gulf War. August 1, 1990, through date to be prescribed by Presidential proclamation or law.

These dates are supplied strictly for reference. Compensation benefits are available to wartime and peacetime era veterans.

Records Review

A claim for compensation requires documentation that a disability is related to the veteran's military service directly, presumptively, via aggravation of a preexisting condition, or secondary to an already service connected disability. Many veterans feel that their current medical records will suffice to document a disability and, when compared to their service medical records, the claim will be granted. In rare occurrences this may be true, but most will find it's not quite that easy!

Arjun-MK-1

As an example, we shall propose the veteran sustained a severe back strain on active duty for which he sought treatment. X-rays were negative so medical personnel treated the back with heat, massage and pain medication. After several weeks of continued treatment the pain decreased and the veteran returned to full duty. Twenty years later, after thousands of dollars of chiropractic treatment and numerous prescriptions for pain killers, the veteran feels that his current back pain is a result of the incident in service. He obtains his chiropractic records, and submits them with a claim for benefits, secure in the knowledge that his service medical records will document the previous injury in service, and the benefits will be granted!

The veteran submits to a VA examination and six months later receives his decision. To his dismay, the claim has been denied. The narrative of the decision explains that, while the veteran was treated in service for a back condition, the injury in service was acute and transitory in nature, and completely resolved prior to discharge. The veteran has provided proof of a current back condition, but no relationship was established between the previously mentioned injury in service and the current disability. The examiner has rendered an opinion that there is no relationship between the current back condition and the injury in service. The veteran is then informed of his right to appeal the decision. Case closed!

The previous example happens thousands of times a year throughout the country, yet can be completely avoided with some relatively simple preparation:

• Upon receipt of service medical records, the veteran should determine what the claimed disabilities are, and review the records thoroughly. He or she should then document in a separate log the dates of treatment, where it took place, the type of treatment rendered, any medication prescribed and what tests were given, including x-rays, MRIs, EKGs etc. The veteran should also document the events leading up to the injury. Was it during the accomplishment of regular duties, physical training, an off base incident, a physical altercation, a sporting event, a motor vehicle accident, as a result of combat, etc.? Any type of medical treatment given off base should also be documented.

B24

Buddy Statements

If the veteran has maintained contact with other service members he or she served with, who know about the injury or condition the veteran is claiming, they should attempt to obtain a "buddy statement" from them in support of the claim. This statement should consist of what was observed as to any incidents witnessed, decrease in performance, physical symptoms, knowledge of treatment or hospitalization, etc.. Speculation as to the cause of the condition in medical terms should be avoided unless the writer is a medical professional.

An acceptable letter would say something like, "I observed Cpl. John Jones get struck by a jeep at Camp Lejeune in March of 1973. I visited him at the base hospital several times over the next month. After his release from the hospital he was on profile and had a noticeable limp on his left side. He was unable to lift more than a few pounds due to the pain in his back. I served with Cpl. Jones until May of 1974 after which he was discharged. His limitations continued for the entire time we served together following the accident."

Apache

An example of a poorly worded and speculative letter is "I observed John Jones get hit by a jeep in 1973 at Camp Lejeune. He was hospitalized for nearly a month. This is the reason his back hurts today." The writer has no basis for his opinion that the current back condition is due to the auto accident in service.

Family members, friends and spouses can also write as to the changes in the veteran either physically or mentally as long as they knew him or her both before, and after, service. Once again, medical speculation should be avoided.

Ensure any "buddy statement" is signed and dated and includes the full name and address of the writer and that the veteran is clearly identified in the narrative of the letter.

Postmarked letters written on active duty can be used to establish the existence of a claimed condition in service, as can newspaper articles or photographs of observable conditions. The veteran must be clearly identified in this type of evidence.

Medical Records

Just as in a court case, the more evidence in the veterans favor, the better. The stronger the evidence, the more likely a positive outcome will be the result. Medical evidence in support of any claim for disability is vital. The VA requires the veteran to establish the existence of a disability prior to processing a claim. Normally, the veteran should provide medical documentation of the disability as part of the initial claim package.

VA medical records are available to the Regional Office at any time. The veteran just has to make them aware of the existence of these records. On the VA claim form 21-526, which is the form necessary to file for compensation benefits, the veteran should list the dates of treatment, which VA facility treated him or her, and what specific disability they were seen for. This triggers the VA's "Duty to Assist" and they will obtain these records and associate them with the claim. VA from 21-526 is obtained from any Veterans Service Officer, or via *http://www.va.gov/vaforms*

For treatment outside the VA system, VA form 21-4142 is normally used. This is a release of information which will allow the VA to request the medical records from a private physician or hospital. In order to provide a complete medical picture, several 21-4142s may be required. The objective is to obtain any pertinent medical information available from the date of discharge to the present. If a dozen different medical providers treated the veteran for the claimed conditions, then a dozen 21-4142s should be submitted. The form itself is available through a Veterans Service Officer or at *http://www.va.gov/vaforms.*

CH-46

In many cases, the veteran is already in possession of pertinent medical records via discharge summaries, treatment notes, prescription forms, etc. This information should be copied and sent to the VA Regional Office, with the veteran's information clearly displayed on each page of the submission. This will prevent the information from being lost in the VA system, which happens quite often.

Employment records may contain pertinent medical evidence if an initial physical was required for hiring. Many employers require annual physicals as well. The veteran may have to acquire these records on his or her own as form 21-4142 may not be effective in obtaining them.

Many claimants will submit medical information discovered

while searching the internet, feeling it describes exactly what is happening to them. This information is very limited in value. The internet is available to everyone, and anyone can render an opinion on any issue. Unfortunately many will take these frivolous opinions as gospel, and submit them as "proof" to the Department of Veteran's Affairs. This "proof" is then easily discarded by the VA as unsubstantiated and irrelevant. Any internet documents have to be obtained from a reputable source, and should consist of general information regarding studies on progression of disease, secondary complications from medication, effects on the internal systems due to physical disability, etc.

Cobra

A much better option is for the veteran to take any medical information obtained through internet research and discuss it with his or her physician. This can be valuable in obtaining what is referred to as a "nexus statement".

Nexus Statements

A nexus statement is basically an informed opinion rendered by a medical professional in support of the veteran's claim. The VA's standard of proof is fifty/fifty in favor of the veteran. In other words, if all evidence is equal, the tie goes to the veteran. An opinion obtained from a medical professional should, at a minimum, contain the words "at least as likely as not". Even better is "more likely than not", or "the claimed condition is definitely associated with the incident on active duty". Wording consisting of phrases such as "it is possible" or "it could be" are not considered favorable evidence and should be avoided.

A proper nexus statement is normally rendered by the veteran's treating physician, one who has known the veteran for several years, and is familiar with the veteran's claimed conditions. The veteran may also seek the assistance of a specialist in the field, with credentials that the Department of Veteran's Affairs would find extremely hard to dismiss. A nexus statement can also be obtained from other medical professionals such as nurses, psychologists, chiropractors, mental health counselors, audiologists, physician's assistants, and dental technicians, as long as the claimed condition deals with the specialty they are trained in. It doesn't make sense for a dental technician to render an opinion on a mental health condition, as the VA would not consider them an expert in the field. A veterans service officer may also be helpful in establishing the acceptable format for a nexus. Once a template is written, the medical professional will have a guide for his or her opinion statement.

Once it is determined which medical professional will be approached for the nexus statement, all of the research previously accomplished now comes in to play. The medical professional should be provided with the pertinent pages of the service medical records pertaining to the disability, any other medical records from VA or civilian facilities, the written log of the history and progression of the

Aircraft Carrier

condition, and any internet research which is relevant to the claim. It is extremely important that this material is reviewed by the medical professional, and any opinion rendered state that he or she has performed this review, with a list of the material provided to them. The reason it is so important is that the rating specialist who will be deciding whether to grant compensation will be inclined to take the word of the VA examiner who will also render an opinion. The ratings specialist will dismiss the opinion rendered in the nexus statement because the VA examiner had reviewed the claims file, including the service medical records, and the medical professional associated with the nexus statement based his or her opinion on the history provided by the veteran. By ensuring that service medical records and post discharge medical information were reviewed and stating that the medical professional has done so, the ratings specialist cannot easily ignore the nexus statement. A favorable outcome will be more likely with the evidence reviewed by the medical professional properly documented.

At this point it should be mentioned that any statement obtained in support of the claim from a doctor or other medical professional may come with a required fee for services. Many veterans will state that they simply cannot afford this fee, and give up any attempt for this type of evidence. There is an old saying that "in order to make an omelet you need to break a few eggs" which applies in this situation. The question the veteran needs to ask him or herself is, "For the money this opinion will cost me, what is the possible reward?" Remember, VA compensation is a monthly benefit, which is generally paid for the rest of the veteran's lifetime. A fee of several hundred dollars paid for a favorable nexus statement could lead to thousands or hundreds of thousands of dollars over the coming years. There are, of course, no guarantees that the VA will grant compensation benefits, but if the nexus statement will "put the veteran over the top", it will be worth it in the long run.

The veteran also has the option of requesting a nexus opinion from a VA physician. It is entirely up to that physician if they will write such a statement, but no harm comes from asking. If a VA physician renders a favorable opinion, it will come at no cost to the veteran.

Once the medical professional has reviewed the veteran's records, the opinion should be rendered after stating how long the individual has been treating the veteran for the claimed condition, any symptoms and secondary conditions

Frigate

associated with the disability, occupational, recreational and social problems caused by the condition, and any special restrictions placed on the veteran (i.e. diet, wearing a brace, cannot drive, etc.). Any x-ray, MRI, EKG or other specialized tests should be documented and the diagnosis stated. Finally, the incident or treatment in service should be specifically cited, and the relationship between the current condition and the veteran's military service related with the minimum standard of "at least as likely as not" (i.e. the veteran's current lumbar spine condition is at least as likely as not due to the automobile accident at the Alameda Naval Air Station is March of 1974). The reason and basis for the medical opinion should be specifically stated in the nexus, (i.e. the veteran was treated at the base hospital for a separated left shoulder as a result of a training accident at Fort Ord in 1965. A physical examination and x-ray evidence show severe arthritic changes at the site of the previous injury). Any additional medical reference material used in arriving at the opinion rendered should be specifically cited in the conclusion of the narrative.

The medical professional's name, address and credentials should be clearly stated on the page, and the veteran's name and claim number/social security number displayed at the top of the document.

It is important to note that a nexus statement for a psychiatric condition will take a different format. In addition to noting the veteran's history, the medical professional must render a diagnosis (PTSD, Dysthymic Disorder, Depression, Schizophrenia, etc.) and include a global assessment of functioning (GAF). This is a comparison of the social and occupational functionality of the veteran compared to the "normal" person. A typical GAF score for a veteran with Post Traumatic Stress Disorder will run somewhere in the range of 40-65. The Department of Veterans Affairs does not rate the veteran's disability strictly on the GAF, but it does play a huge part in the final outcome of the claim. The diagnosis of the condition is essential. A VA examiner typically spends fifteen minutes to half an hour with the veteran during the examination. This is simply not enough time to establish the existence of the claimed disorder, and certainly not enough time to assess the impact of the disability on the veteran's social and occupational activities. Relying on the compensation and pension examination for diagnosis of a claimed mental condition is futile. Time should be spent with a competent mental health professional who will take the time to properly assess and diagnose the veteran's psychiatric disability.

CV-22 Osprey

What Type of Conditions Can Be Claimed?

The first time a claim for disability compensation is filed with the Department of Veterans Affairs, the veteran must submit VA Form 21-526. Normally, assistance would be sought through a Veteran's Service Officer accredited with the VA. If the veteran decides to forego this type of help and go it alone, Form 21-526 can be found online at *http://www.va.gov/vaforms.*

The option to file the application for benefits online is available through the VONAPP program at *www.va.gov*, or the claim can be directly mailed to the regional office, but assistance with the claim is highly recommended. Veterans should take the time to sit down with a Veteran's Service Officer and discuss what conditions should be claimed. This can prevent problems with the claim as the process moves forward.

Super Hornet

Certain conditions are not considered disabilities by the Department of Veterans Affairs. Examples include high cholesterol, alcoholism, substance abuse, tobacco addiction, decrease in vision due to aging, genetic conditions and personality disorders. There is little point in filing for a disability which has no chance of being granted. The veteran should concentrate on those conditions which led to some of the disabilities previously listed. In many cases, veterans with psychiatric conditions developed addiction to tobacco, alcohol and controlled substances due to "self-medication". Certain genetic conditions may have been aggravated by the veteran's service, such as spondylosis of the back. Vision problems may possible be related to diabetes. Personality disorders in service may have been misdiagnosed (during the period 1940-1980 it seems every psychiatric problem in the military was a personality disorder), and a claimable condition such as schizophrenia or post traumatic stress disorder may be the true diagnosis. The objective of the claim is to have a favorable decision no matter the path taken to establish a condition as service connected.

There are five different methods to obtain service connection for a claimed condition, each of which will be discussed in detail in the following pages.

Direct Service Connection

The most common means of establishing disability compensation for a claimed condition is "Direct service connection". This simply means that the disability was incurred on active duty and continues to affect the ability to obtain and maintain employment now. In most, but not all, cases, treatment was rendered at base or field medical facilities and service medical records reflect any medical diagnosis.

AT38 Talon

Basically, any condition which was not labeled as "acute" is subject to direct service connection. Some common examples would include residuals of gunshot or shrapnel wounds, broken bones, back strain, shoulder separation, knee conditions, pes planus, puncture wounds and cuts requiring sutures, amputations, open and closed head injuries, arthritic conditions , recurrent diseases such as diabetes, cardio vascular disease, pulmonary conditions, malaria, multiple sclerosis, chronic headaches, ulcers, reproductive system disorders, genital conditions, hemorrhoids, various cancers, skin conditions, etc. The key to direct service connection is that the condition was diagnosed or treated while on active duty, and still has residual effects today.

Some conditions may not have been treated on active duty, but can be directly service connected. The most common condition in this category is hearing loss with associated tinnitus (ringing in the ears). Prior to the 1980's, a veteran was normally given a whisper test upon discharge to determine any degree of hearing loss. This consisted of the examiner standing about fifteen feet away and whispering to the veteran. If the veteran heard what the individual was saying, he passed! This test was certainly not accurate or scientific in any way. Most veterans are initially afflicted with high frequency hearing loss, which the whisper test did not begin to assess. In point of fact, hearing loss is the most common disability associated with military service.

Other conditions may have been untreated due to combat. Many service members found it "inconvenient" to drop their weapons and run to a field hospital, and in many cases no medic or corpsman was available on the field of battle. The Federal Court of Appeals for Veteran's Claims *(www.uscourts.cavc.gov)* has determined that a veteran's claim for combat injuries must be taken for fact unless that claim is inherently incredible. In other words, if it is conceivable that the injury took place while the veteran was engaged in combat with enemy forces, the claim is considered "well grounded" and the Department of Veterans Affairs must assist with the development of the claim. Further proof need only consist of a medical diagnosis of a current condition, and a relationship established between the combat injury and the current disability. This relationship should be established via a nexus statement as previously discussed.

In some cases, treatment may have occurred at civilian medical facilities. This may have occurred during extended leave periods or while awaiting orders. In those cases, a request for records from those medical facilities (VA Form 21-4142) should be submitted. Police reports and buddy statements also assist in establishing that the claimed disability began during the time period the veteran contends.

It's important to point out that every claimed condition must have been determined to be in the line of duty. If punitive action (Court Martial, non-judicial punishment, etc.) took place, the injury would normally not be in the line of duty and compensation would be denied. Examples would be injuries in bar scuffles with police involvement, injuries resulting from controlled substance abuse, and fallout from domestic violence. Line of duty determinations are available in the serviceman's personnel and medical records.

Many veterans develop theories as to why a certain condition must be related to service, and then rely on the VA to prove their theory is correct. This is absolutely the wrong way to go about validating the theory, as

B25 Mitchell

the VA will almost certainly deny the claim. If there is no mention of a condition in service medical records, it falls to the veteran to prove the theory is true! The VA will not take the veterans word for it.

An example of application of a theory in obtaining service connection for a disability is as follows:

The veteran was involved in painting a shaft alley onboard a carrier while on active duty. The veteran used an epoxy paint which gave off toxic fumes. Makeshift ventilation was provided as there was no regular ventilation shafts to the compartment. The veteran was provided a respirator to filter the fumes, and a shipmate was to check on him regularly. Several hours later, the veteran is found passed out in the shaft alley, overcome by fumes. He is rushed to sick bay and revived, and returned to duty several hours later. The incident is then all but forgotten.

Several years later, the veteran develops chronic obstructive pulmonary disease (COPD). The veteran does not smoke, has never worked in a hazardous environment, and lives in the country, far from any areas of heavy smog. After thinking back on his experiences, he determines the only incidence of any type of toxic exposure to his lungs was in the shaft alley onboard ship. He files a claim with the VA for his COPD with a detailed statement as to why he should be service connected for the condition. He receives a denial letter six months later, as the condition was not found to have occurred on duty and was not related to service!

Any theory for service connection must be validated with the opinion of at least one medical professional, preferably two or more. There may be scientific studies already in existence which deal with this

LC-130 Hercules

type of situation, but the evidence must be specific to the veteran's claim. Remember the rules for service connecting a claim directly are an incident in service (passing out due to toxic fumes), a current condition (COPD), and a relationship shown between the two. The third element of a service connected claim is missing. The veteran may have presented a plausible theory, but there must be at least one nexus statement validating the theory, and a VA examiner is unlikely to do so. The veteran

19

should obtain the nexus prior to submitting a claim for benefits.

The veteran should not be discouraged if the initial claim for service connection based on a theory is denied, even when nexus statements are provided. It may be that the rating specialist feels that they do not have the authority to grant such a claim, as it falls outside of the rules and guidelines set forth in the Code of Federal Regulations. There is a possibility that such a claim could be granted through the appellate process, as a federally appointed law judge would have the ability to apply their interpretation of the law differently than a Regional Office ratings technician.

Psychiatric Conditions

Many psychiatric conditions are considered to be directly service connected despite manifesting years or even decades after service. Examples of these disabilities include post traumatic stress

LAV-25

disorder (PTSD), dysthymic disorder, and chronic depression. These are known as acquired psychiatric disorders. In truth, the dysthymic disorder and chronic depression are usually part of the post traumatic stress disorder condition which will be the only condition referred to in the following discussion.

The Diagnostic and Statistical Manual of Mental Disorders, Fourth Edition (1994) states:

"The essential feature of Posttraumatic Stress Disorder is the development of characteristic symptoms following exposure to an extreme traumatic Stressor involving direct personal experience of an event that involves actual or threatened death or serious injury, or other threat to one's physical integrity; or witnessing an event that involves death, injury, or a threat to the physical integrity of another person, or learning about unexpected or violent death, serious harm, or threat of death or injury experienced by a family member or other close associate."

Common symptoms of post traumatic stress disorder include hyper vigilance, inability to accept authority, anti-social tendencies, panic attacks, sleep disorders, fits of rage, memory loss, night sweats, intrusive thoughts, suicidal thoughts, flattened affect, and many others. Veterans afflicted with PTSD often turn to substance abuse and alcohol addiction to decrease the effects of the condition. This is referred to as self-medication.

Any diagnosis of PTSD should follow the guidelines set forth is DSM IV (Diagnostic and Statistical Manual of Mental Disorders fourth edition by the American Psychiatric Association), found here:

http://www.ptsd.va.gov/professional/pages/dsm-iv-tr-ptsd.asp

The elements allowing service connection for post traumatic stress disorder are slightly different than for a standard service connected disability. In order to establish service connection for PTSD the veteran must establish that a traumatic incident (or incidents) happened in service, have a current diagnosis of a psychiatric condition, and have a statement relating the current condition to the incident in service. The incident in service will now be referred to as a "stressor".

VA Form 21-0781 is used to document a stressor associated with combat, with 21-0781a used to document stressors associated with personal assault or other trauma. VA Form 21-0960P-3, filled out by a medical professional, will help in relating the stressors to a diagnosed condition, (for depression, etc, use form 21-0960P-2).

B26 Invader

These forms are available through a veteran's service officer or at *http://www.va.gov/vaforms*.

The events used as a stressor must be proven to be factual. Documentation for stressful events in service for those who experienced combat are generally easier to prove than that involving personal assault or other trauma. The receipt of a purple heart, silver star, bronze star with V, combat infantry badge, and various other combat awards is ample proof of the veteran's participation in stressful events while in service. Personnel records will also document the participation in major battles and campaigns. A review of the DD-214 may show any wounds received in combat and participation in major campaigns as well.

If the veteran is in receipt of a combat award, the 21-0781 will be used to give specifics as to the stressful event or events. In cases where the veteran was wounded and in receipt of a purple heart, the veteran need only refer to the award citation which documents the date, locations and sequence of events associated with the award. Combat situations not involving wounds will require a more detailed explanation of the stressor situation. This would include casualties, enemy action, fear of death or disability due to the situation, feelings of helplessness, fear of capture, and fear of the unknown. The stressor statement should be as detailed as possible. The veteran should first write down his recollection of events, set it aside for a few days and read what has been written. Generally details which were not documented in the initial draft will come to mind, and a more complete description of the events will be possible. A stressor statement should never be rushed. Third, fourth and even fifth drafts are recommended.

Slamer

There are veterans who feel that talking or writing about the events leading to post traumatic stress disorder will have them regarded as a "wimp", and somehow less than manly. First of all, none of this information will be made public so no one other than the service officer, mental health professionals and VA rating specialists need know the details. Secondly, the veteran is asking for monthly benefits based on these events. The VA must have a confirmed diagnosis of post traumatic stress disorder in order to grant the benefit, and the diagnosis cannot be rendered unless the stressor statement is revealed to be a true account of events. Unless the details of the stressful situation are revealed, there is no hope of verifying the accuracy of the veteran's account.

Buddy statements and letters from the time period are also helpful in documenting that a stressful event actually occurred. Pictures may or may not be helpful, as, with the passage of time, it may be hard to identify the veteran's participation in the event portrayed in the photograph.

Frigate

A recent change in the law allowing a grant of benefits for PTSD includes the stipulation that if a VA psychiatrist or psychologist accepts the stressor as truthful and factual, the rating specialist should also do so. This allows for an easier path for those who have been treated by VA mental health professionals for months or years prior to filing a claim for the first time. For those who have never sought treatment in the past, the assistance of an outside mental health professional may be required. Unfortunately, the VA psychiatrist or psychologist performing the mental health examination for compensation purposes will spend very little time with the veteran prior to rendering a diagnosis. It is not recommended that the veteran count on the compensation examination for the initial diagnosis of PTSD. In most cases, the diagnosis obtained in that manner will be unsatisfactory.

When no details of the veteran's participation in stressful events is revealed by the DD 214 or personnel records, it may be necessary to fall back on historical records. The VA will generally acknowledge that anyone stationed in Vietnam will have been subject to rocket or mortar attacks, and most of these attacks are easily verified. Veterans of other wars and conflicts who served in combat zones should have little trouble documenting this type of attack. In addition, many service men were temporarily attached to different units due to needs of the service, with little or no documentation provided. Those temporary transfers often resulted in combat action with the enemy. If the veteran can remember the names of friends or fellow servicemen killed in action, this may also be accepted as a stressful event Anyone who became a prisoner of war after capture by the enemy is entitled to service connection for numerous conditions via presumption, which follows an entirely different set of rules and regulations that will be discussed in later pages. The following websites may be helpful in determining the identities of fellow servicemen who died in action or historical records of individual units:

http://www.history.navy.mil/library/online/american%20war%20casualty.htm.

http://thewall-usa.com/

http://www.globalsecurity.org/military/ops/iraq_casualties.htm

http://www.archives.gov/research/arc/ww2/

As stated earlier, additional information may be obtained from morning reports, ships logs, or casualty reports. Standard Form 180 should be used to initiate a search at the National Records Repository:

www.archives.gov/veterans/military-service-records

When a mental health professional outside of the VA system diagnoses PTSD, he or she must refer back to the stressful situation in service and tie the current PTSD diagnosis, at least in part, to the traumatic event on active duty. If this is not done, the claim has little chance of being granted. The veteran should provide as much information as possible to the psychiatrist/psychologist, including a detailed account of the stressful event. It is recommended that the mental health professional review the information presented on VA Form 21-0781, and any supporting documents prior to rendering a written diagnosis. If possible, a Global Assessment of Functioning Score should also be

F-14 Tomcat

attached to the written diagnosis. Any diagnosis rendered must meet the criteria set forth in the aforementioned DSM IV.

Those veterans who are afflicted with PTSD due to other types of traumatic events may have trouble obtaining documentation of a stressful incident. In the case of those veterans filing for a psychiatric disorder due to rape or sexual or physical assault, the incident may have gone unreported. This is not unusual, as the victims of this type of attack often did not report anything to authorities due to shame, fear of reprisals, threats of physical harm or death, or even transfer in an attempt to cover the incident up entirely. Some assaults may have been perpetrated by the spouse, which raises many other issues including loss of income, thoughts of the children, instances of chronic abuse, and others.

Victims of physical and sexual assault may lend credence to their claim by providing copies of personal evaluations or fitreps showing a decline in performance, medical records with treatment for venereal disease or pregnancy tests, letters to home, buddy statements from friends and coworkers marking a change in behavior or personal knowledge of the event and even police reports showing substance abuse, public drunkenness, etc.

Prior to the establishment of the Federal Court of Appeals for Veteran's Claims, many of the personal assault PTSD cases were dismissed for lack of evidence. The Court's actions on several of these claims heightened the VA's duty to assist the claimant, and increased their attention to the sensitive nature of these particular cases. Some proof will always be necessary, but the testimony of the veteran in assault cases is always factored in heavily when the decision is made. VA Form 21-0781a should be submitted with this type of case via a service officer or obtained at *http://www.va.gov/vaforms*.

Other claims for PTSD may involve participation in events such as natural disasters, terrorist attacks, quelling civil unrest, motor vehicle or airline accidents and participation in police actions. These type of claims have stressors which are generally easily verified

KC-135

through newspaper articles, television recordings, police reports, personnel records, and service medical records. In many instances a simple internet search will provide all of the evidence needed to verify a stressor in this type of case.

Some claimants have filed for depression based on simply experiencing failure to adjust to military life, hazing, conscientious objector status, sexual orientation, domestic situations, or inability to meet military fitness standards. This type of claim is difficult, but not impossible to pursue. The key to success is in the mental health professional's assessment. A well written statement accompanying a diagnosis will greatly enhance the veteran's chances of a successful outcome. The veteran should include any written evidence such as evaluations, fitreps, discipline write ups, non-judicial punishment or court martials, counseling reports via the chaplain or a military psychiatrist, statements from friends and family comparing the veteran's personality before and after

P-38

service, and buddy statements from fellow service members. A stressor statement is not part of this type of claim, as there is no specific action or incident causing the condition, but the entire military experience.

Please note the discussion of acquired psychiatric conditions above does not include those conditions which were diagnosed and treated on active duty, only those that developed years later. Psychiatric conditions treated on active duty are claimed following the guidelines for simple direct service connected claims. The development of psychiatric disorders due to the lifestyle changes brought about by service connected disabilities, and not by the military experience itself, are service connected as secondary to the service connected disability as discussed in the next section. How a mental condition is related to service is important in obtaining a successful outcome to the claim.

Secondary Service Connection

Secondary service connected claims refer to those conditions that developed due to a previously service connected condition (or one that will be service connected).

For example, a veteran is afflicted with diabetes on active duty, but treatment consists of pills to control his or her glucose level and no other symptoms are present while in the military. Three years after active duty, the veteran is placed on insulin. Three years after that, the veteran developed neuropathy (loss of feeling) in the lower extremities. Several years later, the diabetes brings about a heart condition, loss of use of the creative organ and loss of kidney function. At age sixty, the veteran experiences severe retinopathy and goes blind. At age sixty-five, the left leg is amputated due to sores becoming gangrenous.

F-111

In the above example, the veteran can directly service connect only the diabetes, which was treated in service. However the natural progression of the disease brought about the neuropathy, heart, renal, and reproductive conditions, and eventually led to the amputation and blindness. All of these conditions are subject to service connection as secondary to the diabetic affliction. It is important to point out that the conditions other than the diabetes are secondary to the diabetes on VA Form 21-526. Otherwise, the rating specialist could deny the secondary conditions as not found in the service medical records. It might be argued that common sense would dictate that secondary conditions should be automatically granted once the primary condition is service connected, but rating specialists are not doctors, and are not allowed to make medical determinations on their own. The claim should always spell out exactly what the veteran is claiming, and how it is related to service, or, in this case, how it is related to the service connected primary condition.

Secondary service connection can occur in many different ways, some of which might not be readily apparent. Suppose the veteran has been placed on steroids for an extended time due to a chronic skin or joint condition. After many years, the veteran may develop an ulcer condition or diabetes as a result of constant steroid use. Worse, the veteran may have masked a serious heart or liver condition because of the steroids. Simply going to the dentist can trigger infections in the bodily systems which the immune system can no longer fight due to the use of steroids. An endocarditis (invasive vegetative growth) of the heart valves could result, with a heart attack to follow.

Glaucoma may eventually lead to total blindness, and will eventually cause some vision loss under the best of circumstances.

Constant use of strong pain killers for service connected conditions can cause deterioration of the liver over time. Some veterans are reduced to hoping for a liver transplant as the liver may be irreparably harmed due to this type of medication.

The veteran may have a severe knee condition due to service, and have developed a constant limp over the years. Eventually, the knee on the other leg may suffer damage due to overcompensating for the service connected knee. The back may have suffered damage due to the awkward gait of the veteran, and foot and toe problems may develop from using only one part of the foot for weight bearing.

Amputation of any limb will cause uneven blood flow though out the body, which forces the heart to work differently. Eventually cardiovascular problems may result, which could be service connected secondary to the amputated limb.

Any serious service connected condition may result in chronic depression due to lifestyle changes forced on the veteran by the disability. The most common instances of a service connected condition resulting in depression are loss of use of a reproductive organ(whether physical loss, erectile dysfunction, hysterectomy, penile deformation, etc.), heart conditions, or amputations. Facial scarring and cancers can also lead to depression in many cases.

B1B

Closed head injuries may lead to chronic headaches, vision problems and tinnitus. Some may even lead to loss of motor function and memory loss.

There has been some success service connecting heart conditions secondary to post traumatic stress disorder. Unfortunately, there is a great deal of resistance to this type of claim. The scientific community disagrees on whether chronic stress can be the cause of a cardiovascular problem and this is reflected in the ratings issued by the VA. This type of claim is normally won through the appellate process.

The key to establishing service connection for a condition secondary to a service connected disability is to establish service connection for the primary condition, and have the relationship between the primary and secondary conditions stated, in writing, by a medical professional. The veteran should never assume that the VA will service connect a secondary condition because "everybody knows that, if you have this condition, this other condition is related to it.". "Everybody knows" is not a valid reason for granting a benefit! The assigned rating technician will want medical verification that the claimed condition is related to the primary condition. The veteran should take the time to obtain a doctor's statement cementing the relationship between the primary and secondary conditions, and submit it with the claim for benefits..

The bottom line is that if a doctor will relate a secondary condition to a service connected condition, and state the reasons and basis for his opinion, there is a good chance for a successful outcome.

It is also important to note that aggravation of an existing condition may be service connected as secondary to a primary service connected condition. An example of this principle is that the veteran has a damaged knee unrelated to military service. The other knee is service connected. Years of limping due to the service connected knee caused additional damage in the non-service connected condition. The other knee may now be service connected even

FCS Mule

if the original injury had nothing to do with service. Of course, a doctor's statement will be necessary to ensure that the VA will acknowledge the worsening of the knee due to the service connected condition.

The following website is an excellent resource for the natural progression of chronic diseases and how secondary conditions may be related to a service connected condition. It will also delineate the secondary effects of common prescribed drugs:

www.merckmanuals.com/professional/index.html

Civilian treatment records are important to a claim for secondary service connection, as the VA will want to establish that the secondary condition began after the primary service connected condition was first diagnosed.

Many claims on a secondary basis have been denied due to treatment for the condition occurring years before the primary condition was noted. Additional discussion of secondary conditions for several specific disability types are found in later pages of this publication.

CV22 Osprey

Service Connection by Aggravation of a Pre-existing Disability

A veteran who has had active, continuous service of six months or more is considered to have been in sound condition when he or she was examined accepted and placed on active duty except for those defects, disorder and infirmities noted during that examination, or where medical evidence establishes the an injury or disease preexisted service.

A preexisting injury or disease will be considered to have been aggravated b active military service where there is an increase in the disability during service unless it is found that the increase in disability is due to the natural progress of the disease.

The usual effects of medical and surgical treatment in service used in treating a preexisting condition will be precluded from service connection, including expected postoperative scars and poorly functioning limbs and organs.

The aggravation of a preexisting condition simply means the condition was noted on the entrance examination and got worse during service.

An example would be as follows:

The veteran injured his left knee while playing football his senior year in high school. Arthroscopic surgery was performed, and the veteran made a full recovery. He enlisted after graduation from high school and went to Army basic training. After basic training, the veteran attended his service school, and four months later was assigned to his unit. While performing his physical training, the left knee suddenly gave out, requiring an additional arthroscopic surgery when x-rays found bone fragments in the joint. The veteran developed a slight limp, and never regained full range of motion in the left knee. In addition, the knee occasionally gave out during the rest of his term of service.

In the example described above, the veteran's knee condition was noted on his entrance examination. He had full range of motion, with no pain or discomfort, and the knee was stable under all conditions. After discharge he was afflicted with restricted range of motion in the knee, wore a

HMMWVY

flexible knee brace, had occasional instability, and constant low level pain in the joint. A comparison of the left knee when the veteran entered service to the condition of the knee upon discharge reveals significant worsening of the pre-existing left knee condition. The veteran's left knee should be rated at a minimum of twenty percent due to aggravation.

Helpful documentation in aggravation cases would include surgical and follow up reports from prior to service, letters from the family doctor regarding the veteran's condition before and after service, and letters from friends and family attesting to the change in the degree of disability.

In a bit of subterfuge, the military would often have the veteran sign a letter stating that a condition existed prior to service, so that he or she could be discharged administratively. Many times this was after years of service! This statement means very little as the veteran was, in most cases, not a medical professional. This was done mainly to prevent having to pay severance pay, or retiring the veteran medically. Unfortunately, many veterans felt that there was no point in ever filing a claim with the VA for disability benefits, as they had already admitted that the condition began prior to service. If the veteran aggravated a condition in service, no matter the time spent on active duty, a claim should be filed for that aggravation, regardless of whether the veteran signed any type of admission that the condition pre-existed service. If the condition was not found on the veteran's entrance examination, a clam should be filed for direct service connection as previously discussed, and, failing that, aggravation of the condition while on active duty. It doesn't matter how a successful outcome is reached, only that service connection is granted for the condition.

As with every other claim for benefits, VA Form 21-526 is required, accompanied by the DD214, a nexus statement from a doctor, and proof of treatment in service. Also included should be statements from friends and family attesting to the severity of the condition before and after service. If available, and medical records regarding the severity of the condition prior to service should be submitted as well.

Service Connection Via Presumption

Presumptive service connection is quite simple. Scientific studies have shown that exposure to certain chemical, biological or radioactive agents will result in a higher incidence of specific types of diseases or other conditions. If the veteran meets the exposure criteria, and has a compensable condition listed as a presumptive disability, service connection will be granted.

Every claim for a presumptive condition should be accompanied by medical records or a release form via VA Form

Hawkeye

21-4142, available at *www.va.gov/vaforms*, which will prove the existence of the claimed condition. It is also imperative that proof of the presumptive criteria for that particular disability is met. (for example Vietnam veterans must have set foot in Vietnam or been a brown water sailor, radiation risk activities must be shown for those conditions associated with radiation exposure, etc.). As with any other type of claim for service connection, it pays to obtain a copy of the service medical records and personnel records. Most required proof of the criteria for presumptive conditions will be found in those documents.

This section will be the largest by far, as each disability related to a specific type of exposure will be listed. Each veteran should search the list for his or her specific disability that matches the exposure criteria. The complete list of these disabilities is found in the Code of Federal Regulations *(http://www.gpoaccess.gov/cfr/)*, and is reproduced in the following pages:

B52

Chronic Diseases Subject to Presumptive Service Connection.

The following diseases shall be granted service connection although not otherwise established as incurred in or aggravated by service if manifested to a compensable degree within the applicable time limit of one year following service in a period of war or following peacetime service on or after January 1, 1947.

- Anemia, primary.
- Arteriosclerosis.
- Arthritis.
- Atrophy, Progressive muscular.
- Brain hemorrhage.
- Brain thrombosis.
- Bronchiectasis.
- Calculi of the kidney, bladder, or gallbladder.
- Cardiovascular-renal disease, including hypertension.

(This term applies to combination involvement of the type of arteriosclerosis, nephritis, and organic heart disease.)

- Cirrhosis of the liver.
- Coccidioidomycosis.
- Diabetes mellitus.
- Encephalitis lethargica residuals.
- Endocarditis. (This term covers all forms of valvular heart isease.)

- Endocrinopathies.
- Epilepsies.
- Hansen's disease.
- Hodgkin's disease.
- Leukemia.
- Lupus erythematosus, systemic.
- Myasthenia gravis.
- Myelitis.
- Myocarditis.
- Nephritis.
- Other organic diseases of the nervous system.
- Osteitis deformans (Paget's disease).
- Osteomalacia.
- Palsy, bulbar.
- Paralysis agitans.
- Psychoses.
- Purpura idiopathic, hemorrhagic.
- Raynaud's disease.
- Sarcoidosis.
- Scleroderma.
- Sclerosis, amyotrophic lateral.
- Sclerosis, multiple.
- Syringomyelia.
- Thromboangiitis obliterans (Buerger's disease).
- Tuberculosis, active.
- Tumors, malignant, or of the brain or spinal cord or peripheral nerves.
- Ulcers, peptic (gastric or duodenal)
- Hansens Disease (leprosy) and tuberculosis allow for an extended presumptive period of three years after discharge. Multiple sclerosis allows a seven year presumptive period.
- If the first manifestations of acute anterior poliomyelitis present themselves in a veteran within 35 days of termination of active military service, it is probable that the infection occurred during service. If they first appear after this period, it is probable that the infection was incurred after service, and service connection for the condition will be denied.

Pavehawk

Tropical diseases.

34

The following diseases shall be granted service connection as a result of tropical service, although not otherwise established as incurred in service if manifested to a compensable degree within the applicable time limit of one year following service in a period of war or following peacetime service.

- Amebiasis.
- Blackwater fever.
- Cholera.
- Dracontiasis.
- Dysentery.
- Filariasis.
- Leishmaniasis, including kala-azar.
- Loiasis.
- Malaria.
- Onchocerciasis.
- Oroya fever.
- Pinta.
- Plague.
- Schistosomiasis.
- Yaws.
- Yellow fever.

M-155

- Resultant disorders or diseases originating because of therapy administered in connection with such diseases or as a preventative measure.

Diseases Specific As to Former Prisoners of War.

If a veteran is a former prisoner of war, the following diseases shall be service connected if manifest to a degree of disability of 10 percent or more at any time after discharge or release from active military, naval, or air service even though there is no record of such disease during service.

- Psychosis.
- Any of the anxiety states.
- Dysthymic disorder (or depressive neurosis).
- Organic residuals of frostbite, if it is determined that the veteran was interned in climatic conditions consistent with the occurrence of frostbite.
- Post-traumatic osteoarthritis.

- Atherosclerotic heart disease or hypertensive vascular disease (including hypertensive heart disease) and their complications (including myocardial infarction, congestive heart failure, arrhythmia).
  - Stroke and its complications.
  - On or after October 10, 2008, Osteoporosis, if the Veteran establishes service connection for posttraumatic stress disorder.

If the veteran is a former prisoner of war and was interned or detained for not less than 30 days, the following diseases shall be service connected if manifest to a degree of 10 percent or more at any time after discharge or release from active military, naval, or air service even though there is no record of such disease during service.

M-60

- Avitaminosis.
- Beriberi (including beriberi heart disease).
- Chronic dysentery.
- Helminthiasis.
- Malnutrition (including optic atrophy associated with malnutrition).
- Pellagra.
- Any other nutritional deficiency.
- Irritable bowel syndrome.
- Peptic ulcer disease.
- Peripheral neuropathy except where directly related to infectious causes.
- Cirrhosis of the liver.
- On or after September 28, 2009, Osteoporosis.

Diseases Specific to Radiation-exposed Veterans.

The diseases listed in this section shall be service-connected if they become manifest in a radiation-exposed veteran.

- Leukemia (other than chronic lymphocytic leukemia).
- Cancer of the thyroid.
- Cancer of the breast.
- Cancer of the pharynx.

- Cancer of the esophagus.
- Cancer of the stomach.
- Cancer of the small intestine.
- Cancer of the pancreas.
- Multiple myeloma.
- Lymphomas (except Hodgkin's disease).
- Cancer of the bile ducts.
- Cancer of the gall bladder.
- Primary liver cancer (except if cirrhosis or hepatitis B is indicated).
- Cancer of the salivary gland.
- Cancer of the urinary tract.
- Bronchioloalveolar carcinoma.
- Cancer of the bone.
- Cancer of the brain.
- Cancer of the colon.
- Cancer of the lung.
- Cancer of the ovary.
- Note: The term urinary tract means the kidneys, renal pelves, ureters, urinary bladder, and urethra.

The term radiation-exposed veteran means either a veteran who, while serving on active duty, or an individual who while a member of a reserve component of the Armed

AC-130 Spectre

Forces during a period of active duty for training or inactive duty training, participated in a radiation-risk activity.

The term radiation-risk activity means:

- Onsite participation in a test involving the atmospheric detonation of a nuclear device.
- The occupation of Hiroshima or Nagasaki, Japan, by United States forces during the period beginning on August 6, 1945, and ending on July 1, 1946.
- Internment as a prisoner of war in Japan (or service on active duty in Japan immediately following such internment) during World War II which resulted in an opportunity for exposure to ionizing radiation comparable to that of the United

States occupation forces in Hiroshima or Nagasaki, Japan, during the period beginning on August 6, 1945, and ending on July 1, 1946.

• Service in which the service member was, as part of his or her official military duties, present during a total of at least 250 days before February 1, 1992, on the grounds of a gaseous diffusion plant located in Paducah, Kentucky, Portsmouth, Ohio, or the area identified as K25 at Oak Ridge, Tennessee, if, during such service the veteran:

• Was monitored for each of the 250 days of such service through the use of dosimetry badges for exposure at the plant of the external parts of veteran's body to radiation; or

F117

• Served for each of the 250 days of such service in a position that had exposures comparable to a job that is or was monitored through the use of dosimetry badges; or

• Service before January 1, 1974, on Amchitka Island, Alaska, if, during such service, the veteran was exposed to ionizing radiation in the performance of duty related to the Long Shot, Milrow, or Cannikin underground nuclear tests.

• The term "day" refers to all or any portion of a calendar day.

• Service in a capacity which, if performed as an employee of the Department of Energy, would qualify the individual for inclusion as a member of the Special Exposure Cohort under section 3621(14) of the Energy Employees Occupational Illness Compensation Program Act of 2000.

• The term atmospheric detonation includes underwater nuclear detonations.

The term onsite participation means:

• During the official operational period of an atmospheric nuclear test, presence at the test site, or performance of official military duties in connection with ships, aircraft or other equipment used in direct support of the nuclear test.

• During the six month period following the official

operational period of an atmospheric nuclear test, presence at the test site or other test staging area to perform official military duties in connection with completion of projects related to the nuclear test including decontamination of equipment used during the nuclear test.

• Service as a member of the garrison or maintenance forces on Eniwetok during the periods June 21, 1951, through July 1, 1952, August 7, 1956, through August 7, 1957, or November 1, 1958, through April 30, 1959.

• Assignment to official military duties at Naval Shipyards involving the decontamination of ships that participated in Operation Crossroads.

M-1

For tests conducted by the United States, the term operational period means:

• For Operation TRINITY the period July 16, 1945 through August 6, 1945.

• For Operation CROSSROADS the period July 1, 1946 through August 31, 1946.

• For Operation SANDSTONE the period April 15, 1948 through May 20, 1948.

• For Operation RANGER the period January 27, 1951 through February 6, 1951.

• For Operation GREENHOUSE the period April 8, 1951 through June 20, 1951.

• For Operation BUSTER-JANGLE the period October 22, 1951 through December 20, 1951

• For Operation TUMBLER-SNAPPER the period April 1, 1952 through June 20, 1952.

• For Operation IVY the period November 1, 1952 through December 31, 1952.

• For Operation UPSHOT-KNOTHOLE the period March 17, 1953 through June 20, 1953.

• For Operation CASTLE the period March 1, 1954 through May 31, 1954.

- For Operation TEAPOT the period February 18, 1955 through June 10, 1955.
- For Operation WIGWAM the period May 14, 1955 through May 15, 1955.
- For Operation REDWING the period May 5, 1956 through August 6, 1956.
- For Operation PLUMBBOB the period May 28, 1957 through October 22, 1957.
- For Operation HARDTACK I the period April 28, 1958 through October 31, 1958.
- For Operation ARGUS the period August 27, 1958 through September 10, 1958.
- For Operation HARDTACK II the period September 19, 1958 through October 31, 1958.
- For Operation DOMINIC I the period April 25, 1962 through December 31, 1962.
- For Operation DOMINIC II/ PLOWSHARE the period July 6, 1962 through August 15, 1962.
- The term occupation of Hiroshima or Nagasaki, Japan, by United States forces means official military duties within 10 miles of the city limits of either Hiroshima or Nagasaki, Japan, which were required to perform or support military occupation functions such as occupation of territory, control of the population, stabilization of the government, demilitarization of the Japanese military, rehabilitation of the infrastructure or deactivation and conversion of war plants or materials.

Stinger

- Former prisoners of war who had an opportunity for exposure to ionizing radiation comparable to that of veterans who participated in the occupation of Hiroshima or Nagasaki, Japan, by United States forces shall include those who, at any time during the period August 6, 1945, through July 1, 1946:
  - Were interned within 75 miles of the city limits of Hiroshima or within 150 miles of the city limits of Nagasaki, or
  - Served immediately following internment in the

areas of Japan involved in atomic blasts or were repatriated through the port of Nagasaki.

Disease Associated with Exposure to Certain Herbicide Agents.

If a veteran was exposed to an herbicide agent during active military, naval, or air service, the following diseases shall be service-connected if the veteran served in country Vietnam during the Vietnam war period (to include brown water sailors), or on or near the DMZ in Korea during the period April 1, 1968 to 31 August 1971, even though there is no record of such disease during service. The veteran must be able to prove that he or she set foot on land in Vietnam, or was a brown water sailor, through river travel or anchoring in harbors within a short distance of land. There is one exception, which is non-hodgkins lymphoma. Compensation for non-hodgkins lymphoma may be obtained by blue water sailors who were in the surrounding coastal waters of Vietnam.

Bradley's

For those who feel that they may fall in the category of "brown water sailor" the VA maintains a list of U.S. Navy and Coast Guard ships associated with military service in Vietnam and possible exposure to Agent Orange based on military records. This evolving list helps Veterans who served aboard ships find out if they may qualify for presumption of herbicide exposure.

The list is found here - http://www.publichealth.va.gov/exposures/agentorange/shiplist/index.asp

Presumptive conditions associated with herbicide exposure are:

- AL amyloidosis
- Chloracne or other acneform disease consistent with chloracne
- Type 2 diabetes (also known as Type II diabetes mellitus or adult-onset diabetes). Form 21-0960E-1 should be used to

document this condition (www.va.gov/vaforms).

- Hodgkin's disease
- Ischemic heart disease (including, but not limited to, acute, subacute, and old myocardial infarction; atherosclerotic cardiovascular disease including coronary artery disease (including coronary spasm) and coronary bypass surgery; and stable, unstable and Prinzmetal's angina) Form 21-0960A should be used to document this condition (www.va.gov/vaforms).

- All chronic B-cell leukemias (including, but not limited to, hairy-cell leukemia and chronic lymphocytic leukemia) VA form 21-0960b should be used to document the existence of this condition. (www.va.gov/vaforms).

B2

- Multiple myeloma
- Non-Hodgkin's lymphoma
- Parkinson's disease. VA form 21-0960b should be used to document the existence of this condition (www.va.gov/vaforms)
- Acute and subacute peripheral neuropathy
- Porphyria cutanea tarda
- Prostate cancer. VA Form 21-0960j-3 should be used to document this condition (www.va.gov/vaforms).
- Respiratory cancers (cancer of the lung, bronchus, larynx, or trachea)
- Soft-tissue sarcoma (other than osteosarcoma, chondrosarcoma, Kaposi's sarcoma, or mesothelioma)

The term soft-tissue sarcoma includes the following:

- Adult fibrosarcoma
- Dermatofibrosarcoma protuberans
- Malignant fibrous histiocytoma
- Liposarcoma
- Leiomyosarcoma
- Epithelioid leiomyosarcoma (malignant leiomyoblastoma)
- Rhabdomyosarcoma
- Ectomesenchymoma
- Angiosarcoma (hemangiosarcoma and

lymphangiosarcoma)
- Proliferating (systemic) angioendotheliomatosis
- Malignant glomus tumor
- Malignant hemangiopericytoma
- Synovial sarcoma (malignant synovioma)
- Malignant giant cell tumor of tendon sheath
- Malignant schwannoma, including malignant

schwannoma with rhabdomyoblastic differentiation (malignant Triton tumor), glandular and epithelioid malignant schwannomas
- Malignant mesenchymoma
- Malignant granular cell tumor
- Alveolar soft part sarcoma
- Epithelioid sarcoma
- Clear cell sarcoma of tendons and aponeuroses
- Extraskeletal Ewing's sarcoma
- Congenital and infantile fibrosarcoma
- Malignant ganglioneuroma

The term acute and subacute peripheral neuropathy means transient peripheral neuropathy that appears within weeks or months of exposure to an herbicide agent and resolves within two years of the date of onset.

The term ischemic heart disease does not include hypertension or peripheral manifestations of arteriosclerosis such as peripheral vascular disease or stroke, or any other condition that does not qualify within the generally accepted medical definition of Ischemic heart disease.

Many veterans are confused as to what ischemic heart disease is. The following is the definition and description of ischemia from the Online Medical Dictionary *(http://medical-dictionary.thefreedictionary.com/ischemia).*

Patriot Launcher

- Ischemia is an insufficient supply of blood to an organ, usually due to a blocked artery.
- Myocardial ischemia is an intermediate condition of coronary artery disease in which the heart tissue is slowly or suddenly starved of oxygen and other nutrients. Eventually, the

affected heart tissue will die. When blood flow is completely blocked to the heart, ischemia can lead to a heart attack. Ischemia can be silent or symptomatic. According to the American Heart Association, up to four million Americans may have silent ischemia and be at high risk of having a heart attack with no warning.

• Symptomatic ischemia is characterized by chest pain called angina pectoris. The American Heart Association estimates that nearly seven million Americans have angina pectoris, usually called angina. Angina occurs more frequently in women than in men, and in blacks and Hispanics more than in whites. It also occurs more frequently as people age—25% of women over the age of 85 and 27% of men who are 80-84 years old have angina.

F-117

People with angina are at risk of having a heart attack. Stable angina occurs during exertion, can be quickly relieved by resting or taking nitroglycerine, and lasts from three to twenty minutes. Unstable angina, which increases the risk of a heart attack, occurs more frequently, lasts longer, is more severe, and may cause discomfort during rest or light exertion.

Ischemia can also occur in the arteries of the brain, where blockages can lead to a stroke. About 80-85% of all strokes are ischemic. Most blockages in the cerebral arteries are due to a blood clot, often in an artery narrowed by plaque. Sometimes, a blood clot in the heart or aorta travels to a cerebral artery. A transient ischemic attack (TIA) is a "mini-stroke" caused by a temporary deficiency of blood supply to the brain. It occurs suddenly, lasts a few minutes to a few hours, and is a strong warning sign of an impending stroke. Ischemia can also affect intestines, legs, feet and kidneys. Pain, malfunctions, and damage in those areas may result.

Ischemia is almost always caused by blockage of an artery, usually due to atherosclerotic plaque. Myocardial ischemia is also caused by blood clots by (which tend to form on plaque), artery spasms or contractions, or any of these factors combined. Silent ischemia is usually caused by emotional or mental stress or by exertion, but there are no symptoms. Angina is usually caused by increased oxygen demand when the heart is working harder than usual, for example, during exercise or during mental or physical stress. According to researchers at Harvard University, physical stress is harder on the heart than mental stress. A TIA is caused by a blood clot briefly blocking a cerebral artery.

Armored AA

Children of Vietnam veterans conceived after the veteran's exposure to herbicides who develop spina bifida may be eligible for monthly benefits. The veteran/and or child must prove that he or she is the veteran's child, that they were conceived after the veteran's exposure to herbicides in Vietnam during the period of the Vietnam War or Korea, and that they have the condition. Children of female Vietnam veterans with certain birth defects may also file for benefits. VA Form 21-0304 *(www.va.gov/vaforms)* is the proper form to use for the benefit, accompanied by medical information verifying the condition

Amyotrophic Lateral Sclerosis

All veterans who served 90 days or more and who develop Amyotrophic Lateral Sclerosis, known as Lou Gehrig's Disease, are eligible for compensation for the disability at any time after service. VA form 21-526 accompanied by medical proof of the disability or medical release form 21-4142 with proof of service (dd214 or equivalent), should be submitted to obtain benefits for this condition. It is also recommended that VA Form 21-2680 and VA Form 21-0960C-2, filled out by a medical professional be submitted with the claim , as special monthly compensation will normally apply in most ALS cases. *(www.va.gov/vaforms)*

Recent legislation has allowed for any veteran service connected for ALS to be rated one hundred percent. It has been recognized that a life span of five years or less is what the veteran is facing after a diagnosis is rendered. The VA will not need to reexamine the veteran unless it is requested that they do so by the claimant.

Claims Based on Chronic Effects of Exposure to Mustard Gas and Lewisite.

Many veterans who think they were exposed to mustard gas and Lewisite were actually exposed to tear gas, which does not meet the presumptive criteria. Many World War II veterans took part in mustard gas tests, and they will be the vast majority of the claimants under this presumption.

Exposure to the specified vesicant agents during active military service under the circumstances described below together with the subsequent development of any of the indicated conditions is sufficient to establish service connection for that condition:

• Full-body exposure to nitrogen or sulfur mustard during active military service together with the subsequent development of chronic conjunctivitis, keratitis, corneal opacities, scar formation, or the following cancers: Nasopharyngeal; laryngeal; lung (except mesothelioma); or squamous cell carcinoma of the skin.

• Full-body exposure to nitrogen or sulfur mustard or Lewisite during active military service together with the subsequent development of a chronic form of laryngitis, bronchitis, emphysema, asthma or chronic obstructive pulmonary disease.

Abrams

• Full-body exposure to nitrogen mustard during active military service together with the subsequent development of acute nonlymphocytic leukemia.

Compensation for certain disabilities due to undiagnosed illnesses

The term Persian Gulf veteran means a veteran who served on active military, naval, or air service in the Southwest Asia theater of operations during the Persian Gulf War.

VA will pay compensation to a Persian Gulf veteran who

exhibits objective indications of a qualifying chronic disability, provided that such disability:

• Became manifest either during active military, naval, or air service in the Southwest Asia theater of operations during the Persian Gulf War, or to a degree of 10 percent or more not later than December 31, 2011; and
• By history, physical examination, and laboratory tests cannot be attributed to any known clinical diagnosis.

For purposes of this section, a qualifying chronic disability means a chronic disability resulting from any of the following (or any combination of the following):

• An undiagnosed illness;
• The following medically unexplained chronic multisymptom illnesses that are defined by a cluster of signs or symptoms:

• Chronic fatigue syndrome;
• Fibromyalgia;
• Irritable bowel syndrome; or
• Any other illness that the VA determines meets the criteria for a medically unexplained chronic multisymptom illness; or
• Any diagnosed illness that the VA determines in regulations prescribed under the Code of Federal Regulations warrants a presumption of service-connection.
• The term medically unexplained chronic multisymptom illness means a diagnosed

F-15

illness without conclusive pathophysiology or etiology, that is characterized by overlapping symptoms and signs and has features such as fatigue, pain, disability out of proportion to physical findings, and inconsistent demonstration of laboratory abnormalities. Chronic multisymptom illnesses of partially understood etiology and pathophysiology will not be considered medically unexplained.

● Objective indications of chronic disability include both signs, in the medical sense of objective evidence perceptible to an examining physician, and other, non-medical indicators that are capable of independent verification.

● Disabilities that have existed for 6 months or more and disabilities that exhibit intermittent episodes of improvement and worsening over a 6-month period will be considered chronic. The 6-month period of chronicity will be measured from the earliest date on which the pertinent evidence establishes that the signs or symptoms of the disability first became manifest.

Minesweeping

● A chronic disability resulting from an undiagnosed illness shall be rated using evaluation criteria for a disease or injury in which the functions affected, anatomical localization, or symptomatology are similar.

Signs or symptoms which may be manifestations of undiagnosed illness or medically unexplained chronic multisymptom illness include, but are not limited to:

- ● Fatigue
- ● Signs or symptoms involving skin
- ● Headache
- ● Muscle pain
- ● Joint pain
- ● Neurologic signs or symptoms
- ● Neuropsychological signs or symptoms
- ● Signs or symptoms involving the respiratory system (upper or lower)
- ● Sleep disturbances
- ● Gastrointestinal signs or symptoms
- ● Cardiovascular signs or symptoms
- ● Abnormal weight loss
- ● Menstrual disorders.

Presumptive Service Connection for Southwest Asia and Afghanistan veterans

A disease listed in this section will be service connected if it becomes manifest in a veteran within one year of service.

The diseases subject to presumptive service connection are:

- Brucellosis.
- Campylobacter jejuni.
- Coxiella burnetii (Q fever).
- Malaria.
- Mycobacterium tuberculosis.
- Nontyphoid Salmonella.
- Shigella.
- West Nile virus.
- Visceral leishmaniasis (has no time limit currently associated with it)

The Southwest Asia theater of operations includes Iraq, Kuwait, Saudi Arabia, the neutral zone between Iraq and Saudi Arabia, Bahrain, Qatar, the United Arab Emirates, Oman, the Gulf of Aden, the Gulf of Oman, the Persian Gulf, the Arabian Sea, the Red Sea, and the airspace above these locations.

Asbestos Exposure

Diseases such as asbestosis, mesothelioma, lung cancer, Chronic Obstructive Pulmonary Disease and fibrosis are not considered presumptive by the Department of Veteran's Affairs. However, if the veteran can prove the potential of asbestos exposure in service, a claim for direct service connection for the condition would generally be successful. Risk activities for asbestos exposure include

PRC-77

lagging preparation and rip out, construction and demolition activities, shipyard work, motor pool work involving brake linings and many others. In general, the use of asbestos in the military was curtailed in the late sixties and early seventies, but there are still some facilities and ships using asbestos to this day. VA form 21-526, a nexus statement and personnel records are essential in this type of claim. The personnel records must prove a reasonable possibility of asbestos exposure through work activity while on active duty.

Hepatitis C

Hepatitis C is another of the semi-presumptive conditions. If the veteran can prove either an infection fo hepatitis A or B in service (or hepatitis non A or B), or significant risk activities, including transfusions, combat injuries, occupational risk of blood to blood transfer (corpsman, medic, doctor) and even unprotected sex, a case may be made for the service connection of the condition. Hepatitis C can take decades to make its presence known, and no test was developed until the late 80's. The veteran should file a claim if any of the risk factors can be proven through medical records, personnel records, buddy statements, etc. It is service connected on a direct basis due to direct blood to blood contact in service, but is presumptive due to the extreme length of the incubation period, and the inability to identify the disease until long after the initial exposure.

Dockback

Traumatic Brain Injury (TBI)

TBI has received a great deal of attention in the past few years and is now one of the predominant types of injuries reported among casualties of Iraq and Afghanistan.

Treatment for repeated concussions among players in the National Football League has allowed for a better understanding of the immediate and long term impact upon the lives of those who received this type of injury.

TBI is defined by the Department of Defense as a traumatically induced structural injury and/or physiological disruption of brain function as a result of an external force that is indicated by new onset or worsening of at least one of the following clinical signs immediately following the event:

- Any period of loss or decreased level of consciousness.
- Any loss of memory for events immediately before or after injury.
- Any alteration in mental state at the time of the injury.
- Neurological deficits that may or may not be transient.

- Intracranial lesion.

There are three main categories of residuals of TBI.

- Physical (headaches, sensory loss, balance, disorder, vomiting, aphasia, tinnitus, etc.).
- Cognitive (attention, memory, judgement, abstract thinking, etc.).
- Behavioral/emotional (depression, anxiety, aggression, impulsivity).

TBI can also cause seizure disorder and increased risk for hormone disorder, Alzheimer's Disease, Parkinson's Disease, and other brain disorders.

Repeated mild TBI's can result in cumulative neurological and cognitive deficits and even death.

For VA disability purposes only a VA or DoD physiatrist, psychiatrist, neurosurgeon, or neurologist can make a diagnosis of TBI.

No other type of claim requires that a VA or DoD physician must diagnose a specific condition. This type of claim cannot be validated by a private physician! The veteran must ensure that his or her VA attending physician (who must be experienced in the TBI field as indicated above) makes a proper diagnosis prior to proceeding.

VA Form 21-526 accompanied by a letter from a DoD or VA physiatrist, psychiatrist, neurosurgeon, or neurologist trained in this field should be submitted to the local Regional Office, or through a veteran's service officer. It is not recommended that this type of

F-4

claim be done through VONAPP as the submitted documents should be screened by a benefits expert to ensure that the diagnosis meets the required criteria. VA Form 21-526 may be obtained at *www.va.gov/vaforms*.

Individual Unemployability

Those veterans who establish a single service connected

disability at the sixty percent rate, or two or more disabilities with a total rating of seventy percent or more with a single disability of at least forty percent may file for individual unemployability if unable to work because of their service connected conditions. The form for this benefit is 21-8940 available through a veteran's service officer or at *http://www.va.gov/vaforms.*

Individual unemployability allows payments and all associated benefits at the one hundred percent rate, despite being assigned a lower disability rating. It is recommended that a letter from a medical professional attesting to the inability to obtain and maintain gainful employment due to service connected disabilities accompany the

F-22

application. Social security records (if available) and a statement from the previous employer are also recommended. Individual unemployability only applies to veteran's who are currently unemployed, or work for very little income in a protected environment. If the veteran is gainfully employed, there is little point in applying for the benefit. This includes owning a business even though very little actual involvement in the work performed is apparent.

Special Monthly Compensation

Many veterans have a great deal of difficulty with the complicated nature of the determination of rates for special monthly compensation. A veteran who feels that he or she is eligible under the provisions for this additional disability payment, should apply for it under the guidelines established for direct service connected compensation. It must be remembered that loss of use of a limb is simply that the extremity is so limited that a prosthetic would allow essentially the same amount of use.

Special monthly compensation follows a graduated scale, which factors in the severity of the disability, the degree of helplessness, and whether a combination of disabilities exist. The designators assigned to special monthly compensation are (k), (l), (m), (n), (o), (p), (r) and (s). There are intermediate designators which essential add ½ of the next higher designator (for example (m1/2). The specific guidelines as listed in the code of federal regulations are reproduced below. This listing is comprehensive and lengthy, but is necessary to understand the complicated nature of determining the exact amount of benefits due a veteran by law:

VA will pay additional compensation to a veteran who, as a result of military service, was afflicted the loss or loss of use of specific organs or extremities. Loss, or loss of use, is described as either an amputation or, having no effective remaining function of an extremity or organ. Loss, or loss of use, is described as either an amputation or, having no effective remaining function of an extremity or organ (i.e. basically the same as having a prosthetic limb).

C-117

The disabilities VA can consider for SMC include:

- Inability to communicate by speech (complete organic aphonia)
- Loss, or loss of use, of a hand or foot
- Immobility of a joint or paralysis
- Loss of sight of an eye (having only light perception)
- Loss, or loss of use, of a reproductive organ
- Complete loss, or loss of use, of both buttocks
- Deafness of both ears (having absence of air and bone conduction)
- Loss of a percentage of tissue from a single breast, or both breasts, from mastectomy or radiation treatment

The VA will pay higher rates for combinations of these disabilities such as loss or loss of use of the feet, legs, hands, and arms, in specific monetary increments, based on the particular combination of the disabilities. There are also higher payments for various combinations of severe deafness with bilateral blindness.

Additional SMC is available if a veteran is service connected for paraplegia, with complete loss of bowel and bladder control.

In addition, if you have other service-connected disabilities that, in combination with the above special monthly compensation, meet certain criteria, a higher amount of SMC can also be considered.

If a veteran is service connected at the 100% rate and is housebound, bedridden, or is so helpless to need the aid and attendance of another person, then payment of additional SMC can be considered. The amount of SMC will vary depending on the level of aid and attendance needed.

The rates payable for those who receive special monthly compensation are available at *http://www.vba.va.gov/bln/21/Rates/comp02.htm.*

Determination of the Applicable Rates are as Follows:

• Determinations must be based upon separate and distinct disabilities. This requires, for example, that where a veteran who had suffered the loss or loss of use of two extremities is being considered for the maximum rate on account of helplessness requiring regular aid and attendance, the latter must be based on need resulting from pathology other than that of the extremities. If the loss or loss of use of two extremities or being permanently bedridden leaves the person helpless, increase is not in order on account of this helplessness. Under no circumstances will the combination of "being permanently bedridden" and "being so helpless as to require regular aid and attendance" without separate and distinct anatomical loss, or loss of use, of two extremities, or blindness, be taken as entitling to the maximum benefit. The fact, however, that two separate and distinct

C-130

entitling disabilities, such as anatomical loss, or loss of use of both hands and both feet, result from a common etiological agent, for example, one injury or rheumatoid arthritis, will not preclude maximum entitlement.

• The maximum rate, as a result of including helplessness

54

as one of the entitling multiple disabilities, is intended to cover, in addition to obvious losses and blindness, conditions such as the loss of use of two extremities with absolute deafness and nearly total blindness or with severe multiple injuries producing total disability outside the useless extremities, these conditions being construed as loss of use of two extremities and helplessness.

• An intermediate rate shall be established at the arithmetic mean, between the two rates concerned.

• Anatomical loss or loss of use of one foot with anatomical loss or loss of use of one leg at a level, or with complications preventing natural knee action with prosthesis in place, shall entitle to the rate between (l) and (m).

• Anatomical loss or loss of use of one foot with anatomical loss of one leg so near the hip as to prevent use of prosthetic appliance shall entitle to the rate under (m).

• Anatomical loss or loss of use of one foot with anatomical loss or loss of use of one arm at a level, or with complications, preventing natural elbow action with prosthesis in place, shall entitle to the rate between (l) and (m).

• Anatomical loss or loss of use of one foot with anatomical loss or loss of use of one arm so near the shoulder as to prevent use of a  prosthetic appliance shall entitle to the rate under (m).

C-141

• Anatomical loss or loss of use of one leg at a level, or with complications, preventing natural knee action with prosthesis in place with anatomical loss of one leg so near the hip as to prevent use of a prosthetic appliance, shall entitle to the rate between (m) and (n).

• Anatomical loss or loss of use of one leg at a level, or with complications, preventing natural knee action with prosthesis in place with anatomical loss or loss of use of one hand, shall entitle to the rate between (l) and (m).

• Anatomical loss or loss of use of one leg at a level, or with complications, preventing natural knee action with prosthesis in place with anatomical loss of one arm so near the shoulder as to prevent use of a prosthetic appliance, shall entitle to the rate between (m) and (n).

• Anatomical loss of one leg so near the hip as to prevent use of a prosthetic appliance with anatomical loss or loss of use of one hand shall entitle to the rate under (m).

• Anatomical loss of one leg so near the hip as to prevent use of a prosthetic appliance with anatomical loss or loss of use of one arm at a level, or with complications, preventing natural elbow action with prosthesis in place, shall entitle to the rate between (m) and (n).

• Anatomical loss or loss of use of one hand with anatomical loss or loss of use of one arm at a level, or with complications, preventing natural elbow action with prosthesis in place, shall entitle to the rate between (m) and (n).

JN-4

• Anatomical loss or loss of use of one hand with anatomical loss of one arm so near the shoulder as to prevent use of a prosthetic appliance shall entitle to the rate under (n).

• Anatomical loss or loss of use of one arm at a level, or with complications, preventing natural elbow action with prosthesis in place with anatomical loss of one arm so near the shoulder as to prevent use of a prosthetic appliance, shall entitle to the rate between (n) and (o).

• Blindness of one eye with 5/200 visual acuity or less and blindness of the other eye having only light perception will entitle to the rate between (l) and (m).

• Blindness of one eye with 5/200 visual acuity or less and anatomical loss of, or blindness having no light perception in the other eye, will entitle to a rate equal to (m).

• Blindness of one eye having only light perception and anatomical loss of, or blindness having no light perception in the other eye, will entitle to a rate between (m) and (n).

• Blindness in both eyes with visual acuity of 5/200 or less, or blindness in both eyes when accompanied by service-connected total deafness in one ear, will afford entitlement to the next higher intermediate rate of if the veteran is already entitled to an intermediate rate, to the next higher statutory rate under, but in no event higher than the rate for (o).

• Blindness in both eyes having only light perception or less, when accompanied by bilateral deafness (and the hearing impairment in either one or both ears is service-connected) rated at 10 or 20 percent disabling, will afford entitlement to the next higher intermediate rate, or if the veteran is already entitled to an intermediate rate, to the next higher statutory rate but in no event higher than the rate for (o).

• Blindness in both eyes rated under (l), (m) or (n), when accompanied by bilateral deafness rated at no less than 30 percent, and the hearing impairment in one or both ears is service-connected, will afford entitlement to the next higher statutory rate or if the veteran is already entitled to an intermediate rate, to the next higher intermediate rate, but in no event higher than the rate for (o).

• Blindness in both eyes rated under (l), (m), or (n), when accompanied by service-connected loss or loss of use of one hand, will afford entitlement to the next higher statutory rate or, if the veteran is already entitled to an intermediate rate, to the next higher intermediate rate, but in no event higher than the rate for (o); or

• Service-connected loss or loss of use of one foot which by itself or in combination with another compensable disability would be ratable at 50 percent or more, will afford entitlement to the next higher statutory rate if the veteran is already entitled to an intermediate rate, to the next higher intermediate rate, but in no event higher than the rate for (o); or

FT-2

• Service-connected loss or loss of use of one foot which is ratable at less than 50 percent and which is the only compensable disability other than bilateral blindness, will afford entitlement to the next higher intermediate rate or, if the veteran is already entitled to an intermediate rate, to the next higher statutory rate, but in no event higher than the rate for (o).

• In addition to the statutory rates payable under (l) through (n) and the intermediate or next higher rate provisions outlined above, additional single permanent disability or combinations of permanent disabilities independently ratable at 50 percent or more will afford entitlement to the next higher intermediate rate or if already entitled to an intermediate rate to the next higher statutory rate but not above the (o) rate. In the application of this subparagraph the disability or disabilities independently ratable at 50 percent or more must be separate and distinct and involve different anatomical segments or bodily systems from the conditions establishing entitlement under (l) through (n) or the intermediate rate

P-51

provisions outlined above. The graduated ratings for arrested tuberculosis will not be utilized in this connection, but the permanent residuals of tuberculosis may be utilized.

• In addition to the statutory rates payable under (l) through (n) and the intermediate or next higher rate provisions outlined above additional single permanent disability independently ratable at 100 percent apart from any consideration of individual unemployability will afford entitlement to the next higher statutory rate or if already entitled to an intermediate rate to the next higher intermediate rate, but in no event higher than the rate for (o). The single permanent disability independently ratable at 100 percent must be separate and distinct and involve different anatomical segments or bodily systems from the conditions establishing entitlement under (l) through (n) or the intermediate rate provisions outlined above.

• Where the multiple loss or loss of use entitlement to a statutory or intermediate rate between (l) and (o) is caused by the same etiological disease or injury, that disease or injury may not serve as the basis for the independent 50 percent or 100 percent unless it is so rated without regard to the loss or loss of use.

• Anatomical loss or loss of use, or a combination of anatomical loss and loss of use, of three extremities shall entitle a veteran to the next higher rate without regard to whether that rate is a statutory rate or an intermediate rate. The maximum monthly payment under this provision may not exceed the amount stated in (p).

• For a veteran who was receiving or entitled to receive

compensation for tuberculosis on August 19, 1968, the minimum monthly rate is $67. This minimum special monthly compensation is not to be combined with or added to any other disability compensation.

• A veteran receiving the maximum rate under (o) or (p) who is in need of regular aid and attendance or a higher level of care is entitled to an additional allowance during periods he or she is not hospitalized at United States Government expense. The regular or higher level aid and attendance allowance is payable whether or not the need for regular aid and attendance or a higher level of care was a partial basis for entitlement to the maximum rate under (o) or (p), or was based on an independent factual determination.

• A veteran receiving compensation at (n) and (o) plus special monthly compensation under (k) who establishes a factual need for regular aid and attendance or a higher level of care, is also entitled to an additional allowance during periods he or she is not hospitalized at United States Government expense.

• The amount of the additional allowance payable to a veteran in need of regular aid and attendance is specified (r)(1). The amount of the additional allowance payable to a veteran in need of a higher level of care is specified in (r)(2). The higher level aid and attendance allowance authorized by (r)(2) is payable in lieu of the regular aid and attendance allowance authorized by (r)(1).

• Those veterans who are service connected for residuals of traumatic brain injury (TBI) may be eligible for a "T" designation if they are:

• In need of regular aid and attendance for the condition but

C-9

• Are not eligible for the higher level of aid and attendance under "R2" and

• Would require hospitalization, nursing home care of other residual institutional care in the absence of regular in-home aid and attendance.

• The special monthly compensation provided by (s) is payable where the veteran has a single service-connected disability rated as 100 percent and has additional service-connected disability or disabilities independently ratable at 60 percent, separate and distinct from the 100 percent service-connected disability and involving different anatomical segments or bodily systems, or is permanently housebound by reason of service-connected disability or disabilities. This requirement is met when the veteran is substantially confined as a direct result of service-connected disabilities to his or her dwelling and the immediate premises or, if institutionalized, to the ward or clinical areas, and it is reasonably certain that the disability or disabilities and resultant confinement will continue throughout his or her lifetime.

B-57 Caberra

As with any other benefit, medical documentation proving the severity of the disability should accompany any claim for special monthly compensation. Direct medical evidence obtained by the veteran may be provided, or the claim should have a medical records release, VA form 21-4142 *(www.va.gov/vaforms)* submitted with it. Any claim for the housebound or aid and attendance benefit should be accompanied by VA form 21-2680 *(www.va.gov/vaforms)* which is to be filled out by a medical professional and verifies the extent of the disabling conditions as to the mobility and self sufficiency of the veteran.

Disabilities Associated with VA Medical Treatment and Vocational Rehabilitation

If the veteran is being treated at a VA medical facility, and is injured by the actions of VA Medical Personnel, and the veteran can prove that the VA was negligent in this action, the condition can be deemed service connected just as if the veteran was on active duty. The standard of proof for any claim involving negligence is extraordinarily high. In this type of claim, the burden of proof falls to the veteran. There is no "benefit of the doubt" involved in this type of action.

If the veteran is enrolled in the vocational rehabilitation program, or performing VA approved work study, and the veteran is injured, service connection may also be established. It is recommended that the veteran consult with a veteran's service officer prior to opening either of these types of claim. In any case, VA form 21-526 is required for requesting disability compensation.

Reopening Previously Denied Claims

Historically, veterans have given up on obtaining service connection for a disability, because the VA denied their claim at some point in the past. In many cases, this was simply because the veteran did not properly develop the claim, and the denial was due to a lack

B-1 Lancer

of evidence. It is always recommended that a veteran obtain the assistance of a veteran's service officer or a guide to obtaining benefits, such as the one at hand.

Generally, in order to reopen a previously denied claim, the veteran must submit new evidence that is material to the claimed condition. This new evidence must be specific to the veteran, not just some internet case study or other similar document. If the evidence is not new and material to the claimed condition, the VA will simply continue the previous denial. However, in the event the claimed condition is a presumptive disability, the veteran may reopen the claim at any time, provided that he or she submits a diagnosis of the claimed condition and meets the required conditions for presumption.

Otherwise, the claim should be approached as if it is a new compensation claim, following the guidelines for direct service connection. The veteran should first file an informal claim, then obtain copies of their service medical records (and personnel records if applicable) from the National Records Center via a Standard Form 180 *(www.archives.gov/veterans/military-service-records.)* and any treatment records after service. After a thorough review of the treatment in service for the applicable disabilities, the veteran should create a written timeline for the first occurrence and later treatment of the claimed condition(s). The veteran may also obtain any applicable internet information such as scientific studies or prescription side effects *(www.merckmanuals.com/professional/index.html),* which are pertinent to their claim. He or she should then discuss the problem with their treating medical professional and, after allowing them to review the evidence, attempt to obtain a nexus statement. The veterans should also obtain "buddy statements" from friends and family who have firsthand knowledge of the effect of the disability on the veteran's occupational and social bearing, and of events leading to the inception of the claimed condition.

Once all evidence is obtained the veteran should then contact a veteran's service officer, the VA Regional Office or go to www.va.gov/vaforms and obtain VA form 21-526b, which is the applicable form for filing for a reopened claim. VA form 21-526b may be filed electronically if desired through the VONAPP program at *www.va.gov*. Remember if filing on line, the evidence must still be mailed to the VA through the postal service, or faxed to the applicable regional office found via the locator at *www.va.gov*. It may be desirable to submit everything at one time, rather than through two different systems. VA form 21-4142 must also be submitted for any medical providers so the treatment records can be released to the VA. It is important that the evidence submitted for the reopened claim is both new, and pertinent to the matter at hand. Treatment records alone do not fit the definition of "new and material" evidence. A nexus statement relating the condition back to service is extremely important in reopening a previously denied claim.

There is no need to submit proof of service, as this is already of record via the previously denied claim. VA form 21-526b is a dramatically shortened version of VA form 21-526 (which needs only be filed once in a veteran's lifetime). In truth, VA form 21-4138 works just as well as 21-526b for reopening a previously denied claim, as would a phone call or any correspondence with the VA on the subject. It is recommended that the

E-8C

veteran use VA Form 21-526b to prevent repeated requests for clarification of the claimed condition, as the 21-526b is very specific and other forms may be too vague to allow the VA to process the claim. The veteran may soon find him or herself overwhelmed with paperwork simply because the proper application for benefits was not initially filed. These repeated requests for clarification and additional records often lead to the veteran losing interest in pursuing the claim.

In the case of a reopened claim, the VA will first rule on whether the claim is reopened, and then decide the claim on the merits of the evidence submitted. It is possible to have the claim reopened, and still have the claim denied. However, under these circumstances the veteran is not appealing whether the claim should be opened, but whether service connection should be granted. This is confusing to some, as they feel any evidence should be towards the issue of service connection when they are actually appealing the denial of opening the claim for consideration.

It must also be noted that a claim for an acquired psychiatric disorder, such as post traumatic stress disorder, is always a new claim. It does not matter if the claim for this type of benefit has been denied once, or a dozen times, as it is attained during the life of the veteran, based on the traumatic event on active duty. The VA can

Air Force One

never refuse to reopen a previously denied claim for this type of psychiatric condition even though they may try. Any denial of an acquired psychiatric condition based on a previously denied claim is improper, and should be appealed immediately, provided the veteran submitted a current diagnosis of the condition with supporting evidence.

In many cases, the veteran was never informed of the VA's decision regarding their initial filing of the claim. In some cases, the VA never complied with their "duty to assist" and obtained all service medical records. In these cases, the claim has not been properly denied, and remains open from the original effective date. This can equate to a large amount of retroactive compensation should service connection be granted. It is recommended that a copy of the entire claims file be requested under the Freedom of Information Act, via form 21-4138.

(www.va.gov/vaforms). The completed form should then be submitted to the applicable regional office. Once the claims file is received, the veteran should contact an accredited Veterans Service Officer for assistance.

Claims for Increased Compensation

Essentially, the only requirement for reevaluation of a service connected condition is to inform the VA that the condition has worsened, and the veteran wishes to be reevaluated for an increased disability rating. Unfortunately, under this scenario, the veteran is counting on the results of a VA examination which may take fifteen minutes to allow a grant of increased compensation. The recommended method is as follows:

EC-130H

The veteran should contact the VA either through VA form 21-4138 or at 1-800-827-1000 and inform them that he or she intends to file a claim for increase. (The form is obtained at *www.va.gov/vaforms* or filed electronically through the VONAPP program.).

Contact the treating medical professional and request all applicable treatment records. It is always a good idea to have a new examination if medical treatment has not been rendered for quite some time.

If available, review the previous VA documentation which granted the disability. Each service connected disability is assigned a rating diagnostic code. If previous VA decisions are unavailable, the veteran can contact the VA at 1-800-827-1000 or a veteran's service officer. The veteran should then take the time to review the criteria for higher disability ratings as listed under that diagnostic code in the Code of Federal Regulations *http://www.gpoaccess.gov/cfr/*

Compare the medical records obtained from the treating medical professional with the criteria listed in the Code of Federal Regulations. If all or most of the criteria have been met, there should be no problem in filing the claim. If not, a conversation with a veteran's service officer is recommended.

If the veteran desires, and can afford it, an examination by a specialist specifically for the purpose of obtaining an increase may be submitted. Any action of this type is strictly up to the veteran's discretion.

The form for requesting reevaluation is VA Form 21-526b. This is available through a veteran's service officer, *www.va.go/vaforms* or electronically through VONAPP. VA From 21-4138 may also be used for this purpose, as long as the veteran claims the condition has worsened and that he or she requests reevaluation. All forms should be submitted to the appropriate regional office *(www.va.gov* and use the locator function). If not already represented, the veteran may submit VA form 21-22 to obtain accredited assistance. VA form 21-4142 should be submitted for any medical records not previously obtained.

Hummer-05

There are certain things to keep in mind when filing a claim for increase:

● The rating for a service connected condition is considered permanent after twenty years at the same rating. Filing for increase after nineteen and a half years, for example, is not a good idea if there is any chance of a decrease in the rating.

● After five years at the same rating, the veteran must show improvement in more than one examination prior to any decrease in that rating.

● When receiving compensation for individual unemployability, a claim for increase which would result in no monetary gain for the veteran would not be wise. The VA could make a determination that the veteran is fit for certain types of employment, and sever the benefit.

VA Claim Timeline

Once a claim for compensation of any type is filed, the following will take place in succession:

- Acknowledgement of the receipt of the claim by the Department of Veterans Affairs (normally a few weeks). Normally the VA will request service medical records at this time. No action by the veteran will be required unless these records are unavailable.

- A Veterans Claims Assistance Act (VCAA) letter will be sent out, requesting any additional information not submitted with the original claim. The VCAA letter can be extremely confusing. It is recommended the veteran obtain the assistance of an accredited service officer, or call the VA at 1-800-827-1000 for help in understanding what is required. This letter requires a rapid response to prevent unnecessarily delaying the claim.

- The VA requests private medical records in support of the claim via previously submitted form 21-4142. Existing social security and VA Hospital records will also be requested at this time.

- The veteran will then be called in for a physical and/or mental examination at the nearest VA hospital facility.

- Once the results of the examination have been obtained, and any private and service medical records have arrived, the claim will be assigned to a ratings specialist to render a decision.

HMMWVAD

- The decision is then reviewed by a senior ratings specialist, and the claim goes to a post-determination team to process any award. Action is then taken to inform the veteran of the results.

Under the best of circumstances, several months are required to process a claim. In some cases the claim may take a year or more to resolve.

In the event of extreme financial hardship or terminal illness, the veteran may have his claim receive expedited processing. Financial hardship will normally have to be proven through supporting documentation (i.e. bankruptcy, shutoff notices, eviction notices, etc.) and terminal illness will require medical documentation of the expected lifespan. This information must then be sent to the local regional office accompanied by VA form 21-4138 *(www.va.gov/va forms)*.

(Under no circumstances should evidence, including medical records, be taken to the compensation examination. Evidence must be submitted to the Regional Office handling the claim, the compensation and pension examiner should not and (hopefully) will not accept evidence for inclusion into the claims file.)

Combat Related Special Compensation

A program run by the Department of Defense called combat rated special compensation (CRSC) may help in obtaining additional monies for those retirees rated at less than fifty percent.. Combat related special compensation is only for wartime associated injuries and conditions. DD Form 2860 is used to apply for CRSC, found here: *http://www.dtic.mil/whs/directives/infomgt/forms/eforms/dd2860.pdf.*

With CRSC, it is possible to receive full military retired pay and VA disability compensation, but the injury has to be combat related. The veteran must provide evidence that proves the injuries were either sustained in combat, were a result of hazardous duty, caused by something utilized in a wartime situation (such as Agent Orange) or in training that simulates war. It is imperative that the veteran have a copy of his or her personnel and service medical records available. These can be obtained through the National Personnel Records Center via Standard Form 180 *(www.archives.gov/veterans/military-service-records)*.

Satellite Dish

Once service records are obtained, follow the procedures for direct service connected compensation. Include any VA decisions which have previously granted service connection for a condition. Remember that DD Form 2860 must be submitted rather than VA form 21-526 and any needed medical records should be submitted directly with the claim, as VA form 21-4142 may not be used for that purpose under the CRSC program. A service officer's assistance is recommended.

CRSC is not a VA program. It is run by the Department of Defense. Contacting the VA about the status of a claim is futile. Veterans requesting status must contact (Army) 1-866-366-2772, (Air Force) 1-800-616-3775, or (Navy) 1-877-366-2772. For more information go to: www.defenselink.mil.

Veterans who have obtained concurrent receipt may not also receive CRSC.

Appeals

This is by no means a detailed discussion of the Appellate process, as that would take an entire book to cover. This is instead a summary of the proper actions to take to ensure an appeal is formalized and perfected.

Every VA decision is subject to an appeal. In addition, the VA must inform the veteran of his or her appellate rights unless a benefit is granted in full (to the maximum allowed by law). The veteran has up to one year of the date he or she was informed of the denial to appeal.

Blue Angels

Upon receipt of a denial, the veteran should file a notice of disagreement on VA form 21-4138 *(www.va.gov/vaforms)*. The Notice of Disagreement must contain the date of the denial and the specific issue(s) the veteran disagrees with. The form should then be sent to the Regional Office which made the decision.

The VA will acknowledge the Notice of Disagreement, and send the veteran a form as to whether he or she would request the regular appeals team process the claim, or a Decision Review Officer (DRO) should be assigned. The veteran should normally select a Decision Review Officer, as that DRO becomes the only person dealing with the claim, rather than several individuals.

The veteran will also be asked if they would like a personal hearing. This is normally an excellent option, which should be utilized in all but the most objective situations requiring additional medical documentation. An example of a purely objective issue is hearing loss. If the veteran's hearing came up normal on the VA examination, there is no helpful testimony which can be given. In this case, test results would have to be obtained which show that a hearing loss exists.

C-130

The DRO issues what is known as a statement of the case. The statement of the case could affirm the previous decision, amend it, or reverse it. The veteran must submit VA Form 9 to the Regional Office upon receipt of the statement of the case if he or she wishes to formally appeal the decision. VA Form 9 will be sent to the veteran with the statement of the case, or may be obtained at *www.va.gov/vaforms*.

After submission of VA Form 9, the claim will be sent to the Board of Veteran's Appeals in Washington DC, where the veteran will once again be asked if he or she desires a personal hearing. The veteran can have a hearing via teleconference at the local Regional Office, or travel to Washington to appear in person. The decision will then be rendered by a Federal Law Judge. The BVA will either affirm the denial, reverse the denial, or remand the claim back to the Regional Office for additional development.

A BVA denial must be appealed within 120 days to the Federal Court of Appeals for Veteran's Claims in Washington . If not, the claim will then be considered finally denied, and no further appeal is possible.

More information on the Board of Veterans Appeals is located here:

www.bva.va.gov

Information on the Federal Court of Appeals for Veterans Claims is located here:

www.uscourts.cavc.gov

Clear and Unmistakable Error

This type of claim is basically the veteran informing the VA they have violated their own rules. Examples include reduction in benefits without due process or an examination, assigning an effective date sometime after a claim was submitted, a severing of individual unemployability with no improvement shown in a service connected condition, etc. A veteran can attempt this type of claim without assistance, but assistance is highly recommended. This claim is for unmistakable error, so no judgment can be involved either by the veteran or the VA. In other words, if the veteran feels the condition should be at twenty percent, and the VA rates it as ten percent, it is generally not a claim for clear and unmistakable error. VA form 21-4138 is used to begin the process (www.va.gov/vaforms).

Hospital and Convalescent Ratings

When a veteran is hospitalized 21 days or more (or under observation at VA expense) for a service connected condition, the condition will be rated at one hundred percent for the period. Normally, the condition will revert to the previously assigned rating following the period of hospitalization.

A discharge summary from the hospital facility should accompany VA Form 21-526b (*www.va.gov/vaforms)* to the VA Regional Office to obtain the benefit.

When surgery is performed upon a service connected condition, the condition will be rated at one hundred percent for the recovery period in monthly increments, with the length of the recovery period detailed in the discharge summary, provided there is at last a one month convalescent period. This total rating would normally be followed by another temporary rating at a lower rate, with an examination scheduled at an appropriate time to allow for stabilization. Following the examination, a permanent rating would be assigned.

Examples of disabilities which may be eligible for hospital ratings include post traumatic stress disorder treatment programs, and stroke recovery programs.

Convalescent ratings may be assigned to any physical disability requiring surgery provided the period of convalescence is one month or more.

A surgical report with discharge summary and Doctor's statement as to the period of convalescence should be submitted with form 21-526b (www.va.gov/vaforms) to the VA Regional Office.

Dependency Indemnity Compensation

Dependency Indemnity Compensation (DIC from this point forward) is a monthly payment to the surviving spouses, children and/or dependent parents of a veteran whose discharge was other than dishonorable and whose death was due to:

• A disease or injury incurred or aggravated in the line of duty while on active duty or active duty for training.

• An injury, stroke, heart attack or cardiac arrest incurred or aggravated in the line of duty while on active duty for training.

• A service connected disability, or condition(s) directly related to a service connected disability.

If the veteran was not service connected for the cause of death, DIC may still be obtained if one of the following requirements are met:

• The veteran was totally disabled due to service connected

conditions for at least ten years preceding his or her death.

• The veteran was continuously rated totally disabled from the date of military discharge and for at least 5 years immediately preceding death.

• The veteran is a former Prisoner of War who was rated totally disabled for service connected causes for a period of at least one year immediately prior to death and who died after 30 September 1999.

Eligibility of DIC dependents is determined by the following:

• The surviving spouse if he or she:

• validly married the veteran before January 1, 1957, OR

• was married to a service member who died on active duty, active duty for training, or inactive duty training, OR

• married the veteran within 15 years of discharge from the period of military service in which the disease or injury that caused the veteran's death began or was aggravated, OR

• was married to the veteran for at least one year, OR

• had a child with the veteran, AND

• cohabited with the veteran continuously until the veteran's death or, if separated, was not at fault for the separation, AND

• is not currently remarried.*

(Note: A surviving spouse who remarries on or after December 16, 2003, and on or after attaining age 57, is entitled to continue to receive DIC).

• The surviving child(ren), if he/she is:

• not included on the surviving spouse's DIC
• unmarried AND
• under age 18, or between the ages of 18 and 23 and attending school or deemed a helpless child prior to age 18.

To file a DIC claim:

• VA Form 21-534 is the proper document used in obtaining the DIC benefit (with the exception of parent's DIC). This is the same form used for the non-service connected pension benefit for survivors (see www.va.gov for non-service connected pension information). If DIC is the only benefit requested, income information requested on the form should not be filled in. The form can be obtained from a local veteran's service officer, the closest VA Regional Office or at www.va.gov/vaforms. It is strongly recommended that VA Form 21-22 selecting a veteran's organization for representation be submitted with the claim. If the veteran had previously been  represented by a service organization, that document becomes invalid with the veteran's death. In claims for DIC, the surviving spouse is now the claimant and should be represented as the claimant. The completed claim forms should then be submitted to the Regional Office for processing along with proof of a valid marriage or birth certificate. Please note that DIC claims go to a centralized location for completion, so, in most cases, the claim will not be completed at the local Regional Office. Regional Offices involved in DIC claim processing are found at www.va.gov using the locator function.

• The *surviving parent(s)* may be eligible for an income-based benefit. It is strongly recommended that the parents consult a veteran's service officer prior to applying for the benefit. It is an income based benefit unlike that for the surviving spouse or child so entitlements such as social security or private pension plans may remove the eligibility for DIC. VA form 21-0514-1 is required for the parent's DIC benefit (www.va.gov/vaforms).

• Payments for DIC vary depending on the date of death. For those veterans deceased prior to 1 January, 1993 the payments are based on military pay grade. For those veterans who died after the aforementioned date the payments are at a set rate. Current payment information can be found at http://www1.va.gov/opa/publications/benefits_book/benefits_cha p12.asp

There are some special allowances for certain conditions regarding a DIC claim:

• If the veteran was totally disabled due to service connected conditions for eight continuous years prior to his or her death, a "kicker" is added to the award.

• There is an additional allowance for dependent children under the age of 18 for the initial two years of entitlement for those awards beginning on or after 1 January 2005.

• There are also additional entitlements if the surviving spouse is housebound of in need of the aid and attendance of another person. In this event VA Form 21-2680 should be filled out by a medical professional and submitted with the claim for benefits (www.va.gov/vaforms).

• In the event the surviving spouse is receiving survivor's benefits from the Department of Defense, only the larger benefit will be received by the claimant (normally DIC).

• The previous chapters in this guide deal with establishing compensation for veterans. The guidelines established in those previous chapters apply to the DIC benefit if the veteran had not previously obtained compensation benefits for the principle cause of death. In every case where the veteran had not met the requirements of total disability listed in the beginning of this

chapter, the surviving spouse must provide proof that the death was "service connected". For instance, if a Vietnam veteran dies of ischemic heart disease, the surviving spouse has only to establish that the cause of death was the aforementioned heart disease, and that the veteran served in Vietnam. The cause of death would normally be on the long form of the death certificate, which would be sufficient proof for VA purposes.

Vietnam service can be verified through the DD214, and , if necessary, service personnel and medical records.

• In most other cases, a claim must be developed just as in establishing compensation for a non-service connected veteran, including medical evidence, military documents and a nexus statement. Please refer to earlier chapters for guidelines in how to accomplish this.

• In DIC cases, the veteran will not be able to speak as to incidents in service, so reliance on records is probable in order to establish the existence of a disability not previously deemed service connected. The veteran's service records may be obtained by the next of kin by requesting them via 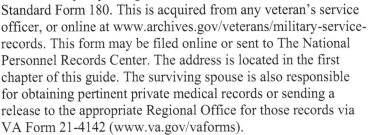 Standard Form 180. This is acquired from any veteran's service officer, or online at www.archives.gov/veterans/military-service-records. This form may be filed online or sent to The National Personnel Records Center. The address is located in the first chapter of this guide. The surviving spouse is also responsible for obtaining pertinent private medical records or sending a release to the appropriate Regional Office for those records via VA Form 21-4142 (www.va.gov/vaforms).

• A little known clause in the Code of Federal Regulations 3.201 states:

"A claimant for dependency and indemnity compensation may elect to furnish to the Department of Veterans Affairs in support of that claim copies of evidence which was previously furnished to the Social Security Administration or to have the Department of Veterans Affairs obtain such evidence from the Social Security Administration. For the purpose of determining the earliest effective date for payment of dependency and indemnity compensation, such evidence will be deemed to have been received by the Department of Veterans Affairs on the date it was received by the Social Security Administration.".

This means simply that a claim for social security is a claim for DIC. This clause in the Code of Federal Regulations may mean additional benefits awarded to a surviving spouse amounting to many years of back pay. In many cases, certain disabilities were not deemed as presumptive conditions by the Department of Veteran's Affairs until scientific studies proved a correlation between conditions the veteran was exposed to and specific disabilities (Please see presumptive conditions previously listed and explained in this book). In this type of claim, the VA must consider the date of the first social security claim after death as the effective date for the DIC benefit, even though years and even decades may have passed. This does not apply to certain conditions in which a specific date for the allowance of benefits is established by law (for example, ALS (Lou Gehrig's Disease) claims cannot be honored prior to the effective date of the law).

Additional Information on Specific Disabilities

There are several specific disabilities which require an in-depth discussion as to the origins, secondary conditions and complications associated with them. Several are presumptive conditions associated with herbicide exposure or service during Iraq-Afghanistan, and others are simply diseases which may have manifested during or shortly after a period of active duty. Some of these conditions were briefly touched upon in previous pages of this publication. A more in depth analysis of the long term ramifications of certain conditions follows:

Diabetes

One of the most common conditions associated with military service is Type 2 diabetes, which is presumptive due to herbicide exposure in Vietnam or Korea, and may be directly service connected if it began while on active duty or within a year of leaving service. Those veterans seeking to obtain service connection for diabetes as a presumptive condition must have set foot in Vietnam during the period 28 February 1961 to 7 May, 1975, or on or near the DMZ in Korea during the period 1 April 1968 to 31 August 1971. Those "brown water" sailors who endured river travel in Vietnam or anchored in harbors within a short distance of land may also be eligible. A complete list of ships that meet the "brown water" criteria may be found at *www.publichealth.va.gov/exposures/agentorange/shiplist/list.asp*

. Those who became diabetic shortly after active duty must provide proof that the diabetes began during the one year period immediately following service, normally through private or VA medical records.

A discussion on diabetes, it's causes and symptoms is readily available on hundreds of on-line medical sites. For detailed information, the veteran should consult with their own physician or other medical professional. A general description of diabetes and how it relates to other disabilities is listed below:

- Type 2 diabetes:

    - Once known as adult-onset or noninsulin-dependent diabetes, is a chronic condition that affects the way the body metabolizes sugar (glucose).

    - With type 2 diabetes, the body either resists the effects of insulin — a hormone that regulates the movement of sugar into your cells — or doesn't produce enough insulin to maintain a normal glucose level. Untreated, type 2 diabetes can be life-threatening.

    - There's no cure for type 2 diabetes, but it can be managed. Treatment may include regulated diet and activities, oral medication or insulin injections. Uncontrolled diabetes may lead to severe complications.

- Nerve damage (neuropathy):

    - Excess blood sugar can affect the capillaries (blood vessels) that nourish the nerves, especially in the lower limbs. This may cause loss of feeling, tingling sensations, or burning pain that starts at the tips of the fingers and/or toes and spreads. Uncontrolled high blood sugar may eventually cause loss of all sense of feeling in the limbs and lead to amputation from undetected infection. Damage to the digestive system nerves may cause development of constipation, nausea, vomiting, or diarrhea. Some men may develop erectile dysfunction due to loss of feeling and depleted blood flow.

- Cardiovascular disease:

• Diabetes increases the chances of acquiring different cardiovascular conditions, including coronary artery disease with chest pain (angina), stroke, narrowing of arteries (atherosclerosis), heart attack and high blood pressure. The chance of stroke is much higher for people with diabetes, and the death rate from heart disease is significantly higher for people with diabetes than for people without it.

• Kidney damage (nephropathy):

• The kidneys filter waste from the blood and may be damaged by diabetes. Significant damage could result in complete kidney failure, dialysis or a possible kidney transplant.

• Hearing and Eye damage:

• Diabetes can damage the blood vessels of the retina (diabetic retinopathy), possibly leading to blindness. Diabetes may increase the risk of other serious vision conditions, such as cataracts and glaucoma. Loss of blood flow to the nerves in the auditory canal may cause hearing damage.

• Skin and mouth conditions:

• Diabetes may leave the skin and gums susceptible to infection.

• Osteoporosis:

• Diabetes can possibly cause osteoporosis by decreasing bone mineral density.

• Alzheimer's disease:

• Type 2 diabetes may increase the risk of Alzheimer's disease and vascular dementia. The poorer the blood sugar control, the greater the risk appears to be. Cardiovascular problems caused by diabetes could contribute to dementia by blocking blood flow to the brain or causing strokes. Too much insulin in the blood may lead to brain-damaging inflammation, or lack of insulin in the brain can deprive brain cells of glucose.

Veterans afflicted with diabetes should become very familiar with the results of their blood tests and urinalysis. These test results will always show where the veteran's fluids are in comparison with the normal range. Attention should be paid specifically to the glucose levels, ketones, and any protein or blood in the urine (indicative of kidney function). Hypoglycemic reactions may occur unless the veteran is vigilant. Frequent eye examinations should be scheduled as retinopathy or other conditions affecting vision are a possible outcome of the disease.

Diabetes by itself is seldom the highest rated disability in a VA rating. Normally, diabetes is rated at ten percent for those veterans who control through diet and twenty percent for those on oral medication or insulin, with higher ratings for an uncontrolled condition which includes restriction of activities, hypoglycemic reactions and hospitalization. It is the secondary conditions that normally result in the highest disability ratings.

Most veterans afflicted with diabetes have some degree of neuropathy. A measurable degree of loss of feeling (via pinprick or other nerve conduction tests) would allow for a compensable rating on each affected extremity. Severe degrees of neuropathy may be rated at much higher levels. Those whose uncontrolled infections in the extremities result in amputation or loss of use of the legs or arms may also be allowed special monthly compensation as discussed in previous pages. Those who suffer from erectile dysfunction due to diabetes may receive special monthly compensation for that affliction.

Blindness or visual impairment due to retinopathy from diabetes may also allow for a disability rating and special monthly compensation.

If the kidneys are affected, the veteran should be rated for loss or loss of use of one or more kidneys as appropriate. Kidney disease may also result in hypertension which should be rated as a separate disability.

Those veterans who are suffering from severe neuropathy, heart conditions or strokes as a result of diabetes may find that the degree of disability is so enormous that several ratings of one hundred percent may apply, resulting in a possible application of the special monthly compensation ratings for housebound or aid and attendance.

If a veteran feels that his or her dementia or Alzheimer's condition may be related to diabetes, it is vital to obtain an expert opinion from a medical specialist concurring with the veteran's hypothesis, to include the reason and basis for the opinion. Normally the Department of Veteran's Affairs will resist relating the cognitive condition with the diabetes unless such an opinion is presented with the claim.

Diabetes is a life altering disease, especially in the more severe cases. Even those who control diabetes with diet and exercise may be forced to avoid food and activities that they have previously enjoyed. Male veterans with the disease may find their sexual activities diminished, or, in some cases, nearly impossible due to erectile dysfunction. Periodic blurring of vision and hypoglycemic reactions may impair work and recreational activities, and slow healing wounds may provide constant irritation. Those who are on insulin are forced to administer their dose every day with blood tests and needles now a normal part of life. Some individuals may be confined to a wheelchair or bedridden, having lost the ability to walk or stand due to neuropathy, or having lost limbs due to diabetes. In severe cases, depression will result, as there is little or no hope of improvement from those suffering from the disease.

In the event that depression develops, it is important to consult with a psychiatrist or psychologist to obtain a diagnosis, and a nexus statement relating the depression to the diabetes. In general, any claimed secondary condition, including heart, neuropathy, kidney, stroke or vision, should have a statement relating them directly to the diabetes.

As discussed in previous pages, the procedures for filing a claim for diabetes are as follows: VA Form 21-526 (for an initial claim), or 21-526b (for those who have previously filed a 21-526 in their lifetime), 21-4142 for any medical records from private providers, and VA Form 21-22 if representation is desired. All forms are available at *www.va.gov/vaforms*. If the veteran is claiming the condition as presumptive due to Vietnam or Korean service with herbicide exposure it should be stated on the claim form. Standard Form 180 may be required for personnel records, unit records, etc. It is strongly suggested that the veteran submit VA Forms 21-0960E-1 (diabetes), 21-0960C4 (neuropathy), 21-0960A-4 (heart), 21-0960J-1 (kidney), 21-0960N-2 (eye condition) 21-0960P-2 and 21-2680 (housebound and aid and attendance), as appropriate, in support of the claim. As always, the veteran may obtain the help of a professional service officer when attempting to file for benefits, and the veteran always has the opportunity to file electronically through the VONAPP program.

Prostate Cancer

The most common type of cancer among modern males is that of the prostate. Prostate cancer is considered a presumptive condition for those set foot in Vietnam during the period 28 February 1961 to 7 May, 1975, or on or near the DMZ in Korea during the period 1 April 1968 to 31 August 1971. "Brown water" sailors in and around the waterways of Vietnam during the war period may also be eligible. Prostate cancer may have also developed on active duty or within one year of service.

Due to the location of the affliction, various side effects and secondary conditions arise with prostate cancer that may not apply to other types of cancer.

A review of various medical sites shows that prostate cancer is a malignant tumor of the prostate, the gland that produces some of the components of semen. The prostate is about the size of a walnut and lies just behind the urinary bladder. A tumor in the prostate interferes with proper control of the bladder and normal sexual functioning. Often the first symptom of prostate cancer is difficulty in urinating. However, because a very common, non-cancerous condition of the prostate, benign prostatic hyperplasia (BPH), also causes the same problem, difficulty in urination is not necessarily due to cancer. Prostate cancer is normally found during periodic rectal exams, or through PSA blood tests.

Cancerous cells within the prostate itself are generally not deadly on their own. However, as the tumor grows, some of the cells break off and spread to other parts of the body through the lymph or the blood, a process known as metastasis. The most common sites for prostate cancer to metastasize are the seminal vesicles, the lymph nodes, the lungs, and various bones around the hips and the pelvic region. The effects of these new tumors are what can cause death.

As of the early 21st century, prostate cancer is the most commonly diagnosed malignancy among adult males in Western countries. Although prostate cancer is often very slow growing, it can be aggressive, especially in younger men.

Prostate cancer is very prevalent among African-Americans, by rates of nearly twice that of other ethnic groups; the mortality rate among African-Americans is also twice as high.

Treatment options for prostate cancer include observation, radiation therapy, surgery, hormone therapy, and chemotherapy. Surgical options include complete removal of the organ, or several more non-invasive procedures which help maintain urinary and reproductive function.

During the period of active cancer, the veteran will normally be rated as one hundred percent disabled by the Department of Veterans Affairs. After treatment is finished, the veteran will continue to receive the one hundred percent rate for six months, and then be reevaluated. At this point, he will be rated as to the residuals of the cancer, unless active malignancy or continued treatment for malignancy is found.

When rating the residuals of the cancer condition, the veteran will have to provide information as to whether he uses protective pads, frequency of urination, and waking intervals at night requiring urination. If a veteran must change pads more than four times a day, he should be rated at sixty percent, two to four times per day is forty percent, less than two twenty percent. A urinary frequency of less than one hour or five or more times per night rates at forty percent, intervals of one to two hours or three to four times per night at twenty percent, or anything less at ten percent. The highest of the above listed instances will be the veteran's assigned rating.

The veteran could also be rated under the criteria for renal dysfunction, which would involve physical issues including lethargy, weakness, exhaustion, anorexia, or weight loss. Once again, only the highest rating will apply.

In addition to the urinary condition, most veterans who have prostate surgery will experience a degree of erectile dysfunction. Some may have no reproductive function available despite surgical or chemical intervention. Those who find sexual intercourse extremely difficult, if not impossible, should file for loss of use of the reproductive organ in an effort to obtain special monthly compensation.

The loss of the ability to have sexual intercourse can be devastating, and may lead to severe depression. There is no doubt that the veteran will have difficulty coping with the condition, especially when in a romantic relationship. Nothing will be quite the same with the sexual element removed, and anger and frustration will result, no matter how hard both partners try to deal with it. The veteran, and his significant other, should obtain professional counseling and psychiatric intervention in order to ease this difficult adaptation in their style and quality of life.

Any depression which occurs as a result of the residuals of the prostate cancer may, in turn, be service connected as secondary to the original condition. The veteran should obtain a nexus statement from his psychiatrist relating the depression to the cancer and its effect on his life, and that of his loved ones.

The procedure for filing a claim for prostate cancer are as follows: VA Form 21-526 (for an initial claim), or 21-526b (for those who have previously filed a 21-526 in their lifetime), 21-

4142 for any medical records from private providers, and VA Form 21-22 if representation is desired. All forms are available at www.va.gov/vaforms. If the veteran is claiming the condition as presumptive due to Vietnam or Korean service with herbicide exposure it should be stated on the claim form. Standard Form 180 may be required for personnel records, unit records, etc. It is strongly suggested that the veteran submit VA Forms 21-0960 J-3 (prostate cancer) and 21-0960P-2(mental disorders), as appropriate, in support of the claim. As always, the veteran may obtain the help of a professional service officer when attempting to file for benefits, and the veteran always has the opportunity to file electronically through the VONAPP program.

If the cancer should metastasize to the lungs, lymph nodes, or other locations, with the prostate as the original site of the affliction, the veteran should file for compensation for the additional cancer sites as secondary conditions. A nexus statement from a medical expert should also be submitted with the claim, confirming the new disability is a result of the original cancer.

ALS

Amyotrophic lateral sclerosis (ALS), also known as Lou Gehrig's Disease, is a condition which causes loss of control of voluntary muscles, characterized by rapidly progressive weakness, muscle atrophy, muscle spasticity, difficulty breathing (dyspnea), difficulty speaking (dysarthria), drooling, and difficulty swallowing (dysphagia). ALS is the most common of the known motor neuron diseases with the exact origin unknown. The disease frequently begins in the hands or feet and spreads to other parts of your body. As the disease progresses, muscles become progressively weaker until no conscious movement is possible. It eventually affects speaking, chewing, swallowing, and breathing. There are a few drugs which help slow the progression of the disease, but, after a few years, the result is generally death.

It must be pointed out that ALS affects the motor neurons for the nerves which control voluntary movements. With ALS, the heart keeps beating, the internal organs including liver, kidneys, etc., still work. Those victims of the disease retain cognitive function and blood flow, but eventually become paralyzed. In some cases the disease will unexpectedly stop spreading and remain in a stagnant state, but these instances are rare.

It has been proven that there is a higher incidence of ALS among veterans than most of the population. The Department of Veterans Affairs has acknowledged this by making the disease a presumptive condition for those who served at least ninety days on active duty. This means that any veteran, regardless of when he or she served, during periods of conflict or during peacetime, is eligible if they served for at least ninety days.

Upon a confirmed diagnosis of ALS, the veteran will automatically receive a rating as one hundred percent disabling. This however, is only the beginning of the eventual disability rating the veteran will receive.

As previously discussed, ALS is a progressive disease that will affect the ability to use the arms, legs, speech, reproductive organs, etc. Every one of these conditions are subject to the special monthly compensation statutes under "loss of use". A veteran with ALS may eventually receive special monthly compensation for loss of use of the arms, legs, reproductive organs, speech, bowels, and bladder. Additional monthly compensation will also apply when the veteran is in need of the aid and attendance of another person for basic daily needs or is completely bedridden. The veteran may finally receive every category of special monthly compensation except for deafness and blindness. This can lead to extremely high disability payments over time. As a rule of thumb, a claim for increase should be filed for each stage of the disease.

Any depression which occurs as a result of ALS may, in turn, be service connected as secondary to the original condition. The veteran should obtain a nexus statement from his psychiatrist relating the depression to ALS and its effect on his life, and that of his loved ones.

Sadly, a veteran with ALS has been afflicted with a condition that will eventually lead to his or her death. There is no point in denial of this fact. Preparations should be made to ensure the veteran's wishes upon death are arranged for, the last will and testament are filed, financial arrangements for the estate are planned, and a full briefing provided to the survivors of the veteran as to what is available from the VA for them when the veteran passes.

The procedure for filing a claim for ALS is as follows: VA Form 21-526 (for an initial claim), or 21-526b (for those who have previously filed a 21-526 in their lifetime), 21-4142 for any medical records from private providers, and VA Form 21-22 if representation is desired. All forms are available at www.va.gov/vaforms. Standard Form 180 may be required for military records as a DD214 will be required for an initial claim. It is strongly suggested that the veteran submit VA Forms 21-0960 C-2 and 21-2680 in support of the claim. The claim should be sent to the nearest VA Regional Office. As always, the veteran may obtain the help of a professional service officer when attempting to file for benefits, and the veteran has the opportunity to file electronically through the VONAPP program.

Multiple Sclerosis

Multiple Sclerosis (MS) is a chronic autoimmune disease of the central nervous system in which gradual destruction of myelin (fat and protein around the nerve endings) occurs in the brain or spinal cord or both, damaging the nerve cells and interfering with the nerve pathways, causing muscular weakness, loss of coordination, speech difficulty, blindness and paralysis. In many cases, the disease is progressive, but some may experience partial or total remission of the condition. The treatment involves medication, possible steroid use, removal of stress factors and lifestyle changes.

The Department of Veterans Affairs has allowed for a special time period of seven years following discharge to allow for the incubation period of multiple sclerosis. If the disease is diagnosed during that period, or if observable symptoms are documented and later diagnosed as multiple sclerosis, service connection will be granted.

The minimum disability rating for MS (thirty percent) is based on the veteran simply having the condition, but if the disease has progressed, special monthly compensation may apply for loss of use of multiple limbs, loss of use of the bowels and bladder, loss of use of the reproductive organs and blindness. In each case, the condition should be recorded and a nexus statement relating the condition to MS provided by a medical professional. A new claim for increase should be filed for each observable progression of the disease. A claim for depression secondary to the MS should also be filed. The veteran may be housebound or in need of the aid and attendance of another person, which entitles them to additional compensation.

 The procedure for filing a claim for MS is as follows: VA Form 21-526 (for an initial claim), or 21-526b (for those who have previously filed a 21-526 in their lifetime), 21-4142 for any medical records from private providers, and VA Form 21-22 if representation is desired. All forms are available at www.va.gov/vaforms. Standard Form 180 may be required for military records which document the onset of the disease. It is strongly suggested that the veteran submit VA Form 21-0960 C-9 in support of the claim and 21-2680 for housebound or aid and attendance benefits. The claim should be sent to the nearest VA Regional Office. As always, the veteran may obtain the help of a professional service officer when attempting to file for benefits, and the veteran has the opportunity to file electronically through the VONAPP program.

Post-Traumatic Stress Disorder and Associated Physical Conditions

Veterans have been suffering from psychological disorders since civilization began. It may have been called shell shock, battle fatigue, a nervous condition, and other more derogatory terms, but it is now commonly known as post-traumatic stress disorder.

Post-traumatic stress disorder (PTSD) is an emotional and behavioral disturbance that may occur after surviving or being exposed to an exceptionally stressful catastrophic event where there is a legitimate fear or death or severe injury. There is no guarantee that PTSD will develop, and many individuals go on with their lives after such events with no psychological difficulties, but some will develop the condition  depending on what happened, and how intense the traumatic event may be. Examples of events from which PTSD may develop include the experiences of those who participated in combat, disaster victims, witnesses to violent death or mutilations, torture victims, a hostage situation, robbery with threat or actual violence, survivors of sexual assault and those who were incarcerated by hostile forces (i.e. Prisoners of War). Word of the death of a close friend or family member may also trigger the condition under certain circumstances.

Development of PTSD is due to not only the intensity, but the duration, frequency and number of traumatic events, and how prepared the individual is who experiences them. Training and a positive outlook can help offset the impact on the individual and help them understand how it is affecting them. Counseling, family support, a focus on the mission at hand and teamwork may help in resisting the long-term effects of the traumatic event as well.

There are many symptoms of PTSD, including:

- Flashbacks
- Intrusive thoughts
- Uncontrolled reactions and anger
- Avoidance of crowds or situations which cannot be controlled
- Lack of concentration and educational failures
- Depressed/Flattened affect or emotional numbness
- Family dysfunction
- Lack of intimacy or marital problems

- Resistance and resentment of authority
- Lack of trust in others with no friends or companions
- Nightmares and night sweats
- Panic attacks and severe anxiety
- Hyper-alertness
- Jumpiness
- Trouble with the law
- Suicidal ideation
- Inability to maintain employment

The proper treatment for PTSD is through medication and counseling by a mental health professional. Many veterans refuse to acknowledge their mental affliction and self-medicate to alleviate their symptoms through the use of illegal drugs or alcohol abuse. Grief, other mental disorders, personal trauma, physical disability, illness and additional traumatic events exacerbate the condition, causing complications in treatment and management of existing PTSD. Many think they have conquered the condition only to have it set off by another traumatic event such as the terrorist attack on September 11, 2001. Many veterans feel that the constant daily stress the suffer results in certain physical ailments which they feel should be service connected as secondary to their PTSD

There are several possible physical illnesses which come about as a result of chronic PTSD. To date, some studies have linked traumatic stress exposures and PTSD to such conditions as cardiovascular disease, diabetes, gastrointestinal disease, fibromyalgia, chronic fatigue syndrome, alcoholism, musculoskeletal disorders, and sleep apnea. A simple search on the internet will bring up case studies associating these conditions with the mental disorder, especially for heart disease and sleep disorders. The Department of Veterans Affairs does not automatically acknowledge any physical condition as a direct result of service connected PTSD. In order to claim the condition secondary to service connected PTSD, the veteran must provide a nexus statement from a reputable expert in the mental health field, stating the direct relationship between the PTSD and the claimed disability. The standard of proof in such a statement is, "at least as likely as not", and the reason and basis of the opinion must be cited. Statements such as "probably a result of" or "could be related" do not meet the necessary standard and the claim will be denied. Further, the death of a veteran by suicide will not be automatically considered due to PTSD without an affirmation by a treating mental health professional meeting the aforementioned standard of proof. Any studies or examples used in deriving a favorable opinion should be specifically stated.

The means by which service connection for PTSD is obtained were discussed in detail earlier in this publication. The veteran should attempt to obtain the diagnosis through a Department of Veterans Affairs mental health professional as that ensures that the "stressor" will be accepted as proof of a traumatic event. The claim should be submitted on VA form 21-526 (original claim) or 21-526b, and accompanied by VA Form 21-0781 for combat situations or 21-0781a for assault, any available nexus statements, buddy or family statements, VA Form 21-0960P-3, and proof of combat awards or citations. A 21-8940 may be submitted if the PTSD and any secondary conditions preclude employment, and VA Form 21-2680 for housebound situations or for those in need of the aid and attendance of another person. All forms are available at *www.va.gov/vaforms*.

Conditions Associated with "Government Experimentation"

Several types of experimental treatment were in use in the military in the post-World War II era. Insulin shock therapy was used on some active duty personnel as a way to combat schizophrenia or coma. Some patients responded positively, but, generally, the treatment led to convulsions, increased risk of psychiatric complications or coma, and left many of the patients extremely obese. There seemed to be no scientific basis for this type of therapy, mainly a "word of mouth" type of treatment. This practice died out by the early 1970's in the United States. A claim for any complications associated with this treatment should be filed as indicated previously, with VA Form 21-526 and a nexus statement from a medical professional associating the claimed condition with the use of insulin shock. The veteran may also wish to file a claim for schizophrenia or concussive residuals if not previously filed.

It may come as a surprise to some that testing of agent orange and other herbicides were tested in the United States and other sites throughout the world prior to use in Vietnam.

Any veteran who wishes to file a claim for exposure must first prove that he or she participated in these tests. A list of the sites where these test were conducted in located at: *http://www.publichealth.va.gov/docs/agentorange/dod_herbicide s_outside_vietnam.pdf*

A request for personnel records and unit records should be sent to the National Personnel Records Center via Standard Form 180. This should help document the possibility of exposure. The veteran must also have one of the conditions associated with herbicide exposure as listed in previous pages of this publication

(diabetes, cancer, ischemic heart disease, etc.). As always VA Form 21-526 (original claim) or 21-526b should be submitted to the Regional Office nearest to the veteran to start the claims process, along with appropriate medical releases via form 21-4142/

There were also incidents involving the use of various hallucinogenic drugs, chemical and bacteriological agents that military personnel were exposed to, either through volunteer participation, or without permission. The use of mustard gas on soldiers in basic training is well documented and described in earlier chapters of this book. The use of soldiers and sailors in atomic tests is also well documented in previous pages. The use of military men as guinea pigs in the testing of various chemical and biological agents is not as well known.

At Edgewood Arsenal in Maryland, from 1955 to 1975, the U.S. Army Chemical Corps conducted classified medical tests. The tests were conducted to determine the effect of certain chemical agents on military personnel and to learn how to defend against them via testing of various protective gear and chemicals designed to counter the adverse effects.

According to the Department of Defense, approximately 7,000 soldiers took part in experiments that involved exposure to more than 250 different chemical agents. Adverse effects over a short time were documented but no plan was in place for tracking the possible long term complications involved in the use of these materials.

According to the information available at *http://www.publichealth.va.gov/exposures/edgewood-aberdeen/index.asp,* The National Academies of Science (NAS) reviewed the potential for long-term health effects from these experiments and did not find any significant long-term physical harm, except for some Veterans exposed to larger doses of mustard agents. NAS published these studies under the title of, "Possible Long-Term Health Effects of Short-Term Exposure to Chemical Agents," in three volumes dated 1982, 1984 and 1985.

In a 2004 follow-up report, "Health Effects of Perceived Exposure to Biochemical Warfare Agents," NAS concluded that post-traumatic stress disorder (PTSD) could occur as a result of "perceived exposure to biochemical warfare agents."

The agents tested included chemical warfare agents and other related agents (inactive substances or placebos such as saline were used):

- Anticholinesterase nerve agents (ex., sarin and common organophosphorus (OP), and carbamate pesticides)
- Mustard agents
- Nerve agent antidotes atropine and scopolamine
- Nerve agent reactivators (ex., the common OP antidote 2-PAM chloride)
- Psychoactive agents (ex., LSD, PCP, cannaboids, and BZ)
- Irritants and riot control agents
- Alcohol and caffeine

There is very little hope of determining exactly which type of agent a veteran was exposed to, or any long term effects, except for the psychological aspects of being used in the experiments. Any veteran who was a "guinea pig" for government testing of chemical and biological agents may have developed a form of Post-Traumatic Stress Disorder from the experience. VA Form 21-526 (original claim) or 21-526b should be submitted along with a diagnosis of Post-Traumatic Stress Disorder from a medical professional relating the condition to the testing while on active duty. The veteran should make every attempt to obtain his or her personnel and medical records via the National Personnel Records Center via Standard Form 180. The forms are all available at *www.va.gov/vaforms.* It would be advisable to acquire the assistance of an experienced veteran's service officer with this type of claim.

Additional Conditions Due to Exposure to Herbicides, etc. (Non-presumptive)

In previous pages the conditions presumptive to herbicide exposure, radiation exposure, service in Iraq and Afghanistan, and others were discussed. Certain conditions which are excluded from the presumptive lists defy logic. For instance,

 cancers of the lungs, trachea and larynx are presumed to be service connected, yet the throat, mouth and nose are excluded. Prostate cancer appears as a presumptive condition, yet the bladder is excluded. The filtering mechanisms of the body, including the liver and kidneys are also excluded. Many veterans who are afflicted with chronic obstructive pulmonary disease feel that herbicide exposure or smoke filled air are the root causes of the disability.

Veterans who feel strongly that a condition is associated with herbicide exposure, service in the Persian Gulf, radiation exposure, etc., should not delay filing a claim for benefits. The lists of presumptive conditions associated with environmental factors change often. A condition excluded today, may appear on the list next year. There should be no hesitation in filing a claim for disability, despite the lack of "presumptive" status.

93

Some veterans have established service connection for conditions they associate with exposure by obtaining nexus statements from noted experts in a particular field. Many cases of esophageal cancer have been granted after herbicide exposure is documented despite the exclusion of that cancer from the list of presumptive conditions. In one example, the veteran consulted a nationally known oncologist from a northern university. The statement provided was so thorough and quoted so many notable sources and studies that the Department of Veterans Affairs really had no choice but to grant the benefit. It can be done, but it is not as easy as for those who can file for a condition already on the presumptive list. An accredited veteran's service officer may be able to help with suggestions on who to see in the local area when attempting to file this type of claim. Even if the claim is denied, it would establish an effective date should the condition be added to the presumptive list in the future. Diabetes and

 ischemic heart condition claims have been granted all the way back to 1985 simply because the veterans afflicted with the disability filed a claim for benefits, even though they were told the claims would be denied when they initially attempted to establish service connection. Hundreds of thousands of dollars in back payments were the result of their efforts. The important thing is to file the claim for benefits, which will allow an earlier date of entitlement for compensation if the specific disability becomes presumptive in the future.

VA Form 21-526 (initial claim) or 21-526b should be filed with the local VA Regional Office along with a statement from a medical specialist relating the disability to the factor that caused the condition (herbicide exposure, radiation, etc.). The veteran should not fear a denial as the claim will most likely be required to advance to the Board of Veteran's Appeals in Washington DC prior to any chance of a grant of service connection. The rating specialists at the local office will stick to the laws as written in the Code of Federal Regulations, while the Law Judges at the Board of Veteran's Appeals have a bit more leeway in deciding claims.

Depression Due to Service Connected Conditions

Service connection for depression and anxiety secondary to a previously service connected condition is a means for obtaining additional compensation benefits which is largely overlooked, and should not be.

Most service connected disabilities bring on some level of depression and many will afflict a veteran with severe symptoms. The degree of disability does not necessarily reflect the psychological effects on the veteran in question. For instance, a one inch scar on the cheek does not really affect the ability to work, receive an education or have a great deal of impact on romantic life. Some male veterans may even feel the scar is an asset while dealing with the opposite sex. It doesn't matter how the scar really got there so much as the story of its origin as related by the veteran. A female veteran is not likely to view a facial scar in the same way. She would generally view it as something ugly, which needs to be hidden as much as possible. Many male veterans would not find the minor disfigurement of a small facial scar depressing in the least, but most female veterans would. This reflects more on the way society views beauty and "manliness" than any disabling effect from the scar, but the psychological impact may be severe.

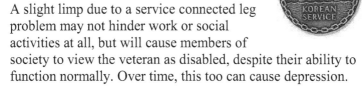

A slight limp due to a service connected leg problem may not hinder work or social activities at all, but will cause members of society to view the veteran as disabled, despite their ability to function normally. Over time, this too can cause depression.

Many disabilities obviously cause depression and anxiety. The loss of a limb will bring about serious changes to the veteran's way of life, and can generally not be hidden from the public. The veteran may actually continue to "feel the limb" for years after amputation, and never truly regain a sense of well-being. Loss of sexual function, at any age, will bring about some degree of depression, more severe, of course, in younger veterans. Many males view the loss of the use of the sexual organs as a loss of their "manhood", with a subsequent lack of interest in social functions and interactions with those of the opposite sex.

A service connected heart condition, even when minimized by stents or bypass surgery, will affect the ability of the veteran to live life the way he or she may have lived it before the surgery. Diet and exercise become a necessary obsession, with certain habits (smoking, drinking) no longer possible. There is always the possibility the heart disease may come back, even worse than before, and the thought of "the big one" is always at the back of the veteran's mind.

A similar problem occurs with cancer, as, even in remission, the worry is that it could always come back. In many cases, cancer causes removal of internal organs or other body parts which not only impact the veteran's way of life, but are severely disfiguring. Depression among cancer victims and survivors is not unexpected.

Some disabilities affect the veteran's ability to work in their chosen field. A veteran with a service connected back condition may find that they can no longer work in a factory setting. Those with diabetes may no longer be able to work on their feet all day. Some with cognitive problems or hearing loss may find themselves not suited for any type of occupation. This can all lead to some degree of depression.

Any veteran who is in constant pain, due to a service connected condition, will be depressed to some degree. It is hard to enjoy life when every waking moment involves sharp or throbbing pain. Those with skin conditions may be so concerned with the itching and burning from the hives or boils that there is no longer any real ability to relax. Many of these types of disabilities will prevent a full night's sleep, contributing to a decreased sense of well-being.

The point is that most service connected disabilities cause depression. The degree of depression will vary with the individual. Just as some combat veterans are not afflicted with

Post-Traumatic Stress Disorder, some veterans will deal with their service connected conditions quite easily. Others will suffer severe psychological problems from what most would consider a minor affliction.

If a veteran feels his or her service connected condition is contributing or is the root cause of depression, it is important to seek the help of a medical professional trained in the field of psychology or psychiatry. The veteran should never count on a VA examination to diagnose their condition, as few examiners would make the necessary diagnosis after one short visit. A series of consultations will be required before the desired "nexus statement" may be obtained. Any statement verifying depression secondary to the service connected condition must state how the condition is impacting the veteran's psychological disposition, and occlude any other factors such as marital difficulties, loss of work, etc., unless they are also a result of the service connected condition.

VA Form 21-0960P-2 would be helpful in obtaining the required information prior to filing a claim on VA Form 21-526b for the secondary condition of depression. Any additional medical records should be requested on VA Form 21-4142. All forms are available at *www.va.gov/vaforms*. The claim may be filed on line through VONAPP or sent to the nearest VA Regional Office with any nexus statements obtained.

One additional note on depression: Some veterans are chronically depressed simply because they were in the military. They did not have horrific experiences, no combat, no disabilities, just loneliness and an inability to fit in. Several female and minority veterans were treated badly and ostracized by their fellow service members due to the prevalent social attitudes in the 50s, 60s and 70s. Many were discharged due to an "adjustment disorder" or were deemed unfit for military service. There will be an inherent prejudice towards this type of claim, but it is possible to succeed if the veteran is sincerely afflicted and a medical professional agrees the condition is due to his or her military experience.

Claims For Exposure to Contaminated Drinking Water at Camp LeJeune and Other Locations

At least two of the water treatment facilities supplying drinking water to the Camp LeJeune Marin base were contaminated with volatile organic compounds.

During the period 1957 to 1987 the level of perchoroethylene in the base drinking water exceeded current acceptable levels.

The Department of Health and Human Service Agency for Toxic Substances and Disease Registry began a study in 2005 which suggests evidence of an association between chronic exposure to perchoroethylene and the following:

- Kidney Cancer
- Esophageal Cancer
- Bladder Cancer
- Breast Cancer
- Lung Cancer

If veteran is afflicted with any of these disabilities and was stationed at Camp LeJeune at any time during the period 1957 to

1987, he or she should file a claim for service connected compensation via VA Form 21-526 *(www.va.gov/vaforms),* accompanied by proof of the disability or a medical release (VA Form 21-4142). The veteran should specifically state that the condition is due to exposure to contaminated drinking water at the Camp.

Several more conditions may have an association with the contaminated water at this location and should be filed for once a diagnosis is rendered.

As of 6 August 2012, veterans who served at Camp LeJeune on active duty for thirty days or more during the period 1 January 1957 to 31 December 1987 may be eligible for medical care for the following conditions:

- Esophageal Cancer
- Breast Cancer
- Kidney Cancer

- Multiple myeloma
- Renal toxicity
- Female infertility
- Scleroderma
- Non-Hodgkins lymphoma
- Lung Cancer
- Bladder Cancer
- Leukemia
- Myelodysplastic syndromes
- Hepatic steatosis
- Miscarriage
- Neurobehavioral effects

It follows that, if these conditions develop, a claim should be filed for compensation on 21-526 (initial claim) or 21-526b, due to exposure to the drinking water. These conditions are not presumptive, so the veteran will generally have to provide a nexus statement relating the consumption of the contaminated water to the current affliction. In most cases, a medical professional will have to be consulted and a statement of this type submitted to ensure that a grant of service connection is possible.

Family members of the veteran who were exposed to the contaminated fluid may also file for medical treatment for these conditions. Studies continue in an effort to determine any possible effects on the veteran's dependents, including unborn children. More information of these studies is available at: http://www.publichealth.va.gov/exposures/camp-lejeune/research.asp

There are currently studies of possible contaminated water at other base locations throughout the world. More information about ongoing surveys and scientific studies is available at *www.va.gov.*

Pain From In Service Connected Musculoskeletal Conditions

Department of Veterans Affairs regulations provide that, in rating disabilities involving the joints of the body, inquiry will be directed to weakened movement, excess fatigability, incoordination and pain on movement. Essentially this means, if pain is experienced when a joint such as a knee or shoulder is moved beyond a certain point, or with repeated movements over time, the rating cannot be deemed non-compensable.

Many veterans carry a disability rating of zero for various service connected injuries. If pain is experienced for any condition involving a major joint or joints, the veteran should immediately file for increase, and ensure that the VA examiner notes his or her pain in movement and how the condition deteriorates over daily activities. The law is clear on this point, but not properly applied during the course of many VA examinations for increase.

When service connection is granted for a knee condition, the veteran should also be aware that separate ratings apply for the same knee when pain and limited motion exist along with instability. The Department of Veterans Affairs has acknowledged that the limited motion and instability are two different types of impairments, even though the same joint is involved. (This is similar to hearing loss and tinnitus in the same ear, separate ratings for the same body part).

VA Form 21-526b should be used to file for increase. The form is found at *www.va.gov/vaforms*.

Parkinson's Disease

Parkinson's disease has been recognized as a presumptive condition for Vietnam service and could develop when a traumatic brain injury or repeated brain injuries occur on active duty.

It is a progressive disease, which advances in stages. The rate of progression will vary with the individual, by may take twenty years or longer.

The normal progression begins with tremors, muscle rigidity, slowness of voluntary movement and postural problems affecting one side of the body. The second stage has the disease spreading to the other side of the body, but ambulation remains unimpaired. In the third state of Parkinson's the symptoms are more pronounced and balance requires additional effort, but the individual may still function without assistance. In the fourth stage the person can stand and walk, but will need assistance with most daily activities. In the last stage, the afflicted person will be bed or wheelchair bound, with constant assistance required.

Initially, the symptoms of Parkinson's may be controlled by medication, but after several years the medication loses its effect. In the late stages or Parkinson's, surgical intervention may be required with electrodes inserted in the brain which will quell some of the uncontrollable tremors. Parkinson's is generally not fatal, and a normal life-span is expected.

Older veterans with Parkinson's may develop dementia after age sixty five. Any veteran with Parkinson's will likely develop depression, especially in the later stages of the disease.

A veteran with Parkinson's due to herbicide exposure should file a claim for the disease through the local VA Regional Office on VA Form 21-526 (initial claim) or 21-526b. The claim should be accompanied by medical proof of the disease and VA Form 21-0960C-1with VA Forms 21-0960P-2 for depression and 21-2680 for aid and attendance if applicable. Proof of service in Vietnam may also be required unless previously established through prior claims. Any additional medical records should be requested via form 21-4142. All forms are available at *www.va.gov/vaforms* and may be filed electronically, if desired, through the VONAPP program.

Veterans who are afflicted with Parkinson's Disease due to a traumatic brain injury will find that it is considered a symptom of the trauma and will be automatically included in the decision under normal circumstances. It never hurts to file the claim separately if desired, as indicated above.

Other Benefits

This publication deals strictly with obtaining compensation benefits for veterans and survivors. There are a multitude of

benefits also available under other VA programs which are
beyond the scope of this guide.
These programs include:

• Non-service connected pension benefits for wartime
veterans (income based)
  • Death pension for surviving spouses of wartime veterans
(income based)
    • Educational benefits for veterans and survivors
    • The home loan guarantee program
    • Death and memorial benefits
    • Vocational rehabilitation
    • Monetary benefits for certain children of Vietnam
Veterans
with birth defects
    • Homeless Veterans assistance
    • Life Insurance
    • Post 9/11 Caregiver benefits
    • Fiduciary services
    • HISA grants for home alteration
    • Small Business Loans
    • Vehicle purchase and modification for totally disabled
service connected veterans

There are also several state and local benefits
available to veterans throughout the country
(including state supported assisted living
facilities). A visit to an accredited veterans
service officer, or the VA Regional Office
may assist an interested individual in
obtaining information on these programs.

The VA website at www.va.gov has a fact
page available for each of these benefits
available via the search function.

Disability Ratings

The disability ratings table is confusing to many veterans. All disability ratings are derived via the combined ratings table in the Code of Federal Regulations, as found here:

http://www.benefits.va.gov/compensation/rates-index.asp#combinedRatingsTable1.

The first given is that a disability rating of ten percent, combined with another ten percent rating is nineteen. When looking at the chart, suppose the veteran has ratings of forty percent, twenty percent and twenty percent. Simple math says that his combined rating is eighty percent. The chart says something different.

Start with the forty percent at the left side of the chart, and look at the twenty percent at the top of the chart. The two ratings intersect at fifty two percent, which is where the next rating is combined. Take the fifty two percent rating on the left side of the chart, and intersect it with the twenty percent at the top of the chart. The two intersect at sixty two percent, which is the combined rating for compensation purposes. The VA only awards compensation by ratings divisible by ten, so, at sixty two percent the rating is brought down to sixty percent which is the rate for which the veteran is awarded benefits.

A few years later, the veteran files for a new disability and is granted an additional ten percent rating. Now the sixty two percent at the left side of the chart is combined with the ten percent at the top of the chart, and the combined result is sixty six percent, which is then rounded up to seventy percent for the compensation award. The chart results are rounded up when combined values ending in five or more are the combined result, and rounded down when less than five. This rounding up or down is only for the final result. As with the example just discussed, if the veteran now receives an additional ten percent disability, the sixty six percent value is used to combine with the new ten percent disability, not the seventy percent value after rounding up. Using the sixty six percent on the left and the ten percent at the top, the new combined rating is sixty nine percent, rounded up to seventy percent for benefit payment. In other words, the additional ten percent did not affect the combined rating value.

Paired disabilities (i.e. two knees, two arms, etc.) allow for additional consideration. Two knees are combined on the rating chart as usual, to arrive at nineteen percent, and ten percent of that value is added (i.e. two percent) for a combined value of twenty one for rating purposes. This is called the bilateral factor.

Special Monthly Compensation rates are derived outside of the Combined Ratings Table. Please refer to the discussion concerning this type of benefit in earlier pages.

"To care for him who shall have borne the battle and for his widow and orphan"

- Abraham Lincoln

Example of a request for a nexus statement
for hearing loss

Dear Dr. Smith,

Mr. John Jones is a veteran of the Vietnam conflict, with active duty service in the U.S. Marine Corps from 8 August 1965 to 7 August 1969.

Mr. Jones was in Vietnam during two separate tours of duty, and served in the infantry during that time.

In January 1969, Mr. Jones was hit by shrapnel when a mortar round exploded several feet from his position. In addition to his wounds, he was knocked unconscious for several minutes. He was treated in the field and spent several days on a Naval Hospital ship prior to returning to duty. We have included documentation of this event via copies of his service medical records and his DD 214 showing receipt of the purple heart. We have also included a copy of the citation accompanying his award.

Since leaving the service, Mr. Jones has been a real estate agent with little or no exposure to loud noise, etc. He does not hunt, and has had no exposure to firearms since leaving active duty. His hearing has gradually worsened over the years, forcing him to obtain hearing aids in 2002. The tinnitus waxes and wanes but has been with him since the day of the incident in service.

Mr. Jones is currently suffering from severe bilateral hearing loss with tinnitus in both ears. He is in receipt of hearing aids which he wears constantly. The Department of Veterans Affairs will likely concede acoustic trauma in service due to the mortar explosion, and his activities in the infantry.

Given the acoustic trauma is fact, as related in the above narrative, is Mr. Jones current hearing loss and tinnitus condition, at least in part, due to the acoustic trauma in service?

If a favorable opinion is possible, please state the reasons and basis of your opinion, and that you have read the service medical records and other documentation provided. The VA standard of proof is "at least as likely as not"

Thank you for your kind attention to this matter.

Sincerely,

Fred Johnson
Dept. Veterans Service Officer

Sample PTSD Request Letter

Dear Dr. Johnson,

Mr. Dan Green is a combat veteran of the Vietnam conflict who has been afflicted with Post Traumatic Stress Disorder.

Included is a copy of his service medical records for your review. During his time in Vietnam you will see treatment for the veteran's wounds, as he was twice hospitalized for shrapnel removal to the right arm and back, and is in receipt of the Purple Heart. Function in the right arm is now extremely limited due to the extent of the injury.

Mr. Green experiences flashbacks to his time in Vietnam on a daily basis. He reports night sweats and terrors, has no close friends, two failed marriages and is estranged from his family. He has been unable to hold a job for over eight years, and now lives solely on social security. He has been arrested on several occasions and incarcerated for assault back in 2002 shortly after the attacks on the world trade center. He avoids crowds, has no hobbies, and his only social function is attendance at group sessions at the vet center. He is an admitted alcoholic, which he used as a form of self-medication due to his psychiatric condition and suffers from rage issues and disdain for authority.

Mr. Green filed a claim for PTSD with the local VA Regional Office, yet was denied as the VA examiner opined that his depressive condition, while similar to PTSD, did not meet the criteria as set forth in DSMIV. This despite the fact that, on at least four other occasions, the veteran has been diagnosed with chronic severe PTSD by VA doctors at the VA Medical Center.

We are requesting your opinion as to whether the veteran's PTSD is, in fact, related to the shell fragment wounds and other incidents in Vietnam, whether it meets the requirements for PTSD as set forth in the Diagnostic and Statistical Manual for Mental Disorders (DSM IV), and your assessment of the severity of his condition to include a global assessment of functioning. We ask that you fill out the attached 21-0960-P3 form to facilitate a favorable decision from the VA rating specialist.

The VA standard of proof is "at least as likely as not", but we hope to have an opinion that far exceeds the minimum necessary.

Thank you for your assistance to this veteran.

Joe Thompson,
Veteran's Service Officer

Sample DD Form 2860

Go to www.va.gov\vaforms to download and print this form.

APPLICATION FOR COMBAT-RELATED SPECIAL COMPENSATION (CRSC)

SECTION I · PERSONAL IDENTIFICATION

1. NAME (Last, First, Middle Initial)

2. MAILING ADDRESS AND CONTACT INFORMATION
   a. STREET (Include apartment number)

2.a. SOCIAL SECURITY NUMBER | b. SERVICE NUMBER (if different)

   b. CITY | c. STATE | d. ZIP CODE

4. DATE OF BIRTH (YYYYMMDD) | 3. RETIRED RANK/PAY GRADE

   e. DAYTIME TELEPHONE NO. (Include area code) | f. E-MAIL ADDRESS (Optional)

6.a. UNIFORMED SERVICE FROM WHICH YOU RETIRED

   b. OTHER UNIFORMED SERVICE(S) IN WHICH YOU SERVED

7. YEAR RETIRED (YYYY)

8. DID YOU RETIRE UNDER MILITARY DISABILITY RETIREMENT PROVISIONS (Chapter 61 of Title 10, U.S. Code)?   YES   NO

SECTION II · PRELIMINARY CRSC CRITERIA
NOTE: You must meet ALL criteria of this section or your application will be denied.

9. ANSWER ONLY THE ONE PART THAT APPLIES TO YOUR RETIREMENT:

   a. FOR REGULAR OR DISABILITY RETIREMENTS ONLY. Do you have 20 or more years of service creditable for the computation of the amount of your retired pay?   YES   NO

   b. FOR NON-REGULAR (RESERVE) RETIREMENT (Retired pay based on points) ONLY. Did you have 7,200 points or more for the computation of retired pay?   YES   NO

10. ARE YOU IN A RETIRED STATUS (i.e., are you on the retired rolls, or have you been transferred to the Fleet Reserve or Fleet Marine Corps Reserve)? Members recalled to, or retained on, active duty are not in a retired status during the period of such recall or retention.   YES   NO

11. ARE YOU ENTITLED TO RETIRED PAY?
   YES - Includes members who have waived military retired pay in order to receive VA disability compensation.
   NO - Includes members who have waived military retired pay in order to credit military service for purposes of a civil service retirement, or for any reason other than to receive disability compensation from the VA.   YES   NO

12. ANSWER ALL PARTS:

   a. Have you been awarded a Purple Heart AND do you receive VA disability compensation based on a combined disability rating of at least 10%?   YES   NO

   b. Do you receive VA disability compensation based on a current combined disability rating of at least 60%?   YES   NO

   c. Have you been awarded a Purple Heart AND did you receive a combined disability rating from the Secretary of a Military Department, as of the date on which you retired from the Military Department, of at least 10%?   YES   NO

   d. Did you receive a combined disability rating from the Secretary of a Military Department, as of the date on which you retired from the Military Department, of at least 60%?   YES   NO

If you answered Yes to Items 9, 10, 11, and at least one part of Item 12, you appear to meet the Preliminary CRSC Criteria and you should continue to Section III. Otherwise, do not complete the application, but you may apply later if your circumstances change and you meet the Preliminary CRSC Criteria.

SECTION III · FINAL CRSC CRITERIA

ORIGIN OF DISABILITIES COMPENSATED BY THE VA

Final CRSC criteria require either a Purple Heart related injury rated at or above 10%, or combat related injuries with a combined rating at or above 60%. If you believe you meet one of these Final CRSC Criteria, you should complete the application. If you do not believe that you meet one of these final criteria, you should not complete the application, but you may apply later if your circumstances change and you believe you meet these Final CRSC Criteria.

In this section list your VA service connected disabilities and provide information and codes that address the disability and how it was incurred. The "Origin of Disability Codes" are fully defined at the end of this section. A four digit Medical Diagnosis Code from the VA Schedule of Rating Disabilities (VASRD) is associated with every VA disability. Begin on the first Section III page with your first disability and use a separate block for each additional disability.

DD FORM 2860 TEST, MAY 2003 | Page 2 of ____ Pages

Sample DD Form 2860 (continued)

Go to www.va.gov\vaforms to download and print this form.

Sample SF Form 180 (continued)

Go to www.va.gov\vaforms to download and print this form.

Standard Form 180 (Rev. 10/16) (Page 2)
Prescribed by NARA (36 CFR 1228.168(b))

Authorized for local reproduction
Previous edition usable.

OMB No. 3095-0029 Expires 10/31/2011

LOCATION OF MILITARY RECORDS

The various categories of military service records are described in the chart below. For each category there is a code number which indicates the address at the bottom of the page to which this request should be sent. Please refer to the Instruction and Information Sheet accompanying this form as needed.

BRANCH	CURRENT STATUS OF SERVICE MEMBER	ADDRESS CODE Personal Record	ADDRESS CODE Service Treatment Record
AIR FORCE	Discharged, deceased, or retired before 5/1/1994	14	14
	Discharged, deceased, or retired 5/1/1994 – 9/30/2004	14	11
	Discharged, deceased, or retired on or after 10/1/2004	1	11
	Active (including National Guard on active duty in the Air Force), TDRL, or general officers retired with pay	1	
	Reserve, retired reserve in nonpay status, current National Guard officers not on active duty in the Air Force, or National Guard released from active duty in the Air Force	2	
	Current National Guard enlisted not on active duty in the Air Force	13	
COAST GUARD	Discharged, deceased, or retired before 1/1/1898	6	
	Discharged, deceased, or retired 1/1/1898 – 3/31/1998	14	14
	Discharged, deceased, or retired on or after 4/1/1998	14	11
	Active, reserve, or TDRL	3	
MARINE CORPS	Discharged, deceased, or retired before 1/1/1905	6	
	Discharged, deceased, or retired 1/1/1905 – 4/30/1994	14	14
	Discharged, deceased, or retired 5/1/1994 – 12/31/1998	14	11
	Discharged, deceased, or retired on or after 1/1/1999	4	11
	Individual Ready Reserve	5	
	Active, Selected Marine Corps Reserve, TDRL	4	
ARMY	Discharged, deceased, or retired before 11/1/1912 (enlisted) or before 7/1/1917 (officer)	6	
	Discharged, deceased, or retired 11/1/1912 – 10/15/1992 (enlisted) or 7/1/1917 – 10/15/1992 (officer)	14	14
	Discharged, deceased, or retired after 10/16/1992	14	11
	Active enlisted, officers (including National Guard and Army Reserve on active duty in the U.S. Army)	7	
	National Guard enlisted and officers not on active duty in Army	13	
NAVY	Discharged, deceased, or retired before 1/1/1886 (enlisted) or before 1/1/1903 (officer)	6	
	Discharged, deceased, or retired 1/1/1886 – 1/30/1994 (enlisted) or 1/1/1903 – 1/30/1994 (officer)	14	14
	Discharged, deceased, or retired 1/31/1994 – 12/31/1994	14	11
	Discharged, deceased, or retired on or after 1/1/1995	10	11
	Active, reserve, or TDRL	10	
PHS	Public Health Service - Commissioned Corps officers only	12	

ADDRESS LIST OF CUSTODIANS (BY CODE NUMBERS SHOWN ABOVE) — Where to write/send this form

1	Air Force Personnel Center HQ AFPC/DPSSRP 550 C Street West, Suite 19 Randolph AFB, TX 78150-4721	6	National Archives & Records Administration Old Military and Civil Records (NWCTB-Military) Textual Services Division 700 Pennsylvania Ave., N.W. Washington, DC 20408-0001	11	Department of Veterans Affairs Records Management Center P.O. Box 5020 St. Louis, MO 63115-5020
2	Air Reserve Personnel Center /DPSSA/B HQ ARPC/DPSSA/B 6760 E. Irvington Place, Suite 4600 Denver, CO 80280-4600	7	U.S. Army Human Resources Command www.hrc.army.mil	12	Division of Commissioned Corps Officer Support ATTN: Records Officer 1101 Wootton Parkway, Plaza Level, Suite 100 Rockville, MD 20852
3	Commander, CGPC-adm-3 USCG Personnel Command 4200 Wilson Blvd., Suite 1100 Arlington, VA 22203-1804	8	Reserved	13	The Adjutant General (of the appropriate state, DC, or Puerto Rico)
4	Headquarters U.S. Marine Corps Personnel Management Support Branch (MMSB-10) 2008 Elliot Road Quantico, VA 22134-5030	9	Reserved	14	National Personnel Records Center (Military Personnel Records) 9700 Page Ave. St. Louis, MO 63132-5100
5	Marine Forces Reserve 4400 Dauphine St. New Orleans, LA 70146-5400	10	Navy Personnel Command (PERS-312E) 5720 Integrity Drive Millington, TN 38055-3120		eVetRecs www.archives.gov/veterans/evetrecs/

Sample VA Form 21-22

Go to www.va.gov\vaforms to download and print this form.

A Guide to Obtaining Veterans Administration Compensation Benefits

Sample VA Form 21-526

Go to www.va.gov\vaforms to download and print this form.

Sample VA Form 21-526 (continued)

Go to www.va.gov\vaforms to download and print this form.

PART VI - MARITAL AND DEPENDENCY INFORMATION - CONTINUED *(If you need additional space, use Item 45 "Remarks")*				
FURNISH THE FOLLOWING INFORMATION ABOUT EACH OF YOUR MARRIAGES *(IF NOT APPLICABLE, WRITE "N/A")*				
29A. DATE AND PLACE OF MARRIAGE	29B. TO WHOM MARRIED	29C. TERMINATED *(Death, Divorce)*	29D. DATE AND PLACE TERMINATED	
MONTH, YEAR / CITY, STATE			MONTH, YEAR	CITY, STATE

FURNISH THE FOLLOWING INFORMATION ABOUT EACH PREVIOUS MARRIAGE OF YOUR PRESENT SPOUSE *(IF NOT APPLICABLE, WRITE "N/A")*				
29A. DATE AND PLACE OF MARRIAGE	29B. TO WHOM MARRIED	29C. TERMINATED *(Death, Divorce)*	29D. DATE AND PLACE TERMINATED	
MONTH, YEAR / CITY, STATE			MONTH, YEAR	CITY, STATE

DEPENDENCY - Dependent Children Information *(If you need additional space, use Item 45 "Remarks")*

FURNISH THE FOLLOWING INFORMATION FOR EACH OF YOUR DEPENDENT CHILDREN

30A. NAME OF CHILD *(First, middle initial, last)*	30B. DATE & PLACE OF BIRTH *(City, state or country)*	30C. SOCIAL SECURITY NUMBER	30D. CHECK EACH APPLICABLE CATEGORY					
			BIOLOGICAL	ADOPTED	STEPCHILD	18-23 YRS. OLD AND IN SCHOOL	SERIOUSLY DISABLED BEFORE AGE 18	CHILD PREVIOUSLY MARRIED
	(Month, day, year) Place:		☐	☐	☐	☐	☐	☐
	(Month, day, year) Place:		☐	☐	☐	☐	☐	☐
	(Month, day, year) Place:		☐	☐	☐	☐	☐	☐

FURNISH THE FOLLOWING INFORMATION FOR EACH OF YOUR DEPENDENT CHILDREN WHO DO NOT LIVE WITH YOU

31A. NAME(S) OF ANY CHILD(REN) NOT IN YOUR CUSTODY	31B. NAME AND ADDRESS OF PERSON HAVING CUSTODY	31C. MONTHLY AMOUNT YOU CONTRIBUTE TO CHILD'S SUPPORT
		$
		$

PART VII - NON-SERVICE CONNECTED PENSION *(If you need additional space use Item 45 "Remarks")*

NOTE: You do not have to submit medical evidence or list disabilities if you are age 65 or older, unless you are housebound, or require the regular assistance of another person.

32. WHAT DISABILITIES PREVENT YOU FROM WORKING? *(List below)*	33. DO YOU NEED THE REGULAR ASSISTANCE OF ANOTHER PERSON OR ARE YOU GENERALLY CONFINED TO YOUR IMMEDIATE PREMISES? ☐ YES ☐ NO

NURSING HOME INFORMATION

NOTE: You may submit a statement by an official of the nursing home that tells us that you are a patient in the nursing home because of a physical or mental disability. The statement should include the monthly charge you are paying out-of-pocket for your care.

34A. ARE YOU NOW IN A NURSING HOME? ☐ YES ☐ NO *(If "YES," complete Items 34B thru 34E)*	34B. NAME AND COMPLETE MAILING ADDRESS OF THE FACILITY	34C. HAVE YOU APPLIED FOR MEDICAID? ☐ YES ☐ NO
34D. DOES MEDICAID COVER ALL OR PART OF YOUR NURSING HOME COSTS OR HAVE YOU APPLIED AND NOT RECEIVED A DECISION? ☐ YES ☐ NO ☐ APPLIED - NOT RECEIVED DECISION	34E. ARE YOU RECEIVING SUPPLEMENTAL SOCIAL SECURITY INCOME (SSI) OR HAVE YOU APPLIED FOR SSI BUT NO DECISION HAS BEEN MADE? ☐ YES ☐ NO ☐ APPLIED - NOT RECEIVED DECISION	

YOU MUST SIGN AND PRINT YOUR NAME AND DATE THIS FORM IN ITEMS 42A THRU 42C ON PAGE 10.

Sample VA Form 21-526 (continued)

Go to www.va.gov\vaforms to download and print this form.

PART III - ACTIVE DUTY SERVICE INFORMATION

NOTE: Please complete the information for each period of active duty. Attach DD214 or other separation papers for all periods of active duty. If you do not have your DD214 form or other separation papers, check the box. ☐

19A. ENTERED INTO SERVICE		19B. SERVICE NUMBER	19C. SEPARATED FROM SERVICE		19D. BRANCH OF SERVICE	19E. GRADE, RANK OR RATING, ORGANIZATION
DATE	PLACE		DATE	PLACE		

PART IV - RESERVE AND NATIONAL GUARD SERVICE INFORMATION

NOTE: Enter complete information for each period of Reserves and National Guard service. Attach any separation papers you have.

20A. ENTERED INTO SERVICE		20B. SERVICE NUMBER	20C. SEPARATED FROM SERVICE		20D. SERVICE STATUS (Reserve, National Guard)	20E. GRADE, RANK OR RATING, ORGANIZATION
DATE	PLACE		DATE	PLACE		

21. IF DISABILITY OCCURRED DURING ACTIVE OR INACTIVE DUTY FOR TRAINING, GIVE BRANCH OF SERVICE AND DATE OF OCCURRENCE

22A. ARE YOU NOW A MEMBER OF THE RESERVES OR NATIONAL GUARD? IF SO, GIVE THE BRANCH OF SERVICE ☐ YES ☐ NO BRANCH

22B. RESERVE STATUS ☐ ACTIVE ☐ RESERVE OBLIGATION ☐ INACTIVE

22C. NAME, ADDRESS AND PHONE NO. OF RESERVE OR NATIONAL GUARD UNIT (if additional space is needed, use Item 45 "Remarks")

PART V - MILITARY RETIRED/SEVERANCE PAY

IMPORTANT - Unless you check the box in Item 25 below, you are telling us that you are choosing to receive VA compensation instead of military retired pay. If it is determined you are entitled to both benefits. If you are awarded military retired pay prior to compensation, we will reduce your retired pay by the amount of any compensation that you are awarded. VA will notify the Military Retired Pay Center of all benefit changes. If you receive both military retired pay and VA compensation, some of the amount you receive may be recouped by VA, or, in the case of Voluntary Separation Incentive (VSI), by the Department of Defense.

23A. ARE YOU RECEIVING MILITARY RETIRED PAY? (If "Yes," complete Items 23C & 23D) ☐ YES ☐ NO

23B. WILL YOU RECEIVE MILITARY RETIRED PAY IN THE FUTURE? (If "Yes," explain, i.e. Future Reserve/National Guard Retirement, Pending MEB/PEB) ☐ YES ☐ NO

23C. BRANCH OF SERVICE

23D. MONTHLY AMOUNT $

24. RETIRED STATUS ☐ RETIRED ☐ TEMPORARY DISABILITY RETIRED LIST ☐ DISABLED RETIRED LIST

25. NO, I DO NOT WANT VA COMPENSATION IN LIEU OF MILITARY RETIRED PAY ☐ (Check box if applicable)

26. HAVE YOU EVER APPLIED FOR OR RECEIVED DISABILITY SEVERANCE/SEPARATION PAY, OR ANY OTHER LUMP SUM PAYMENT FROM THE ARMED FORCES? (If "Yes," list type, amount, date it was received, and the branch of service below) ☐ YES ☐ NO

PART VI - MARITAL AND DEPENDENCY INFORMATION

27A. MARITAL STATUS (If married, complete Items 27B thru 27K) ☐ MARRIED ☐ WIDOWED ☐ DIVORCED ☐ NEVER MARRIED (If never married, skip to Item 30)

27B. SPOUSE'S BIRTHDATE (mo., day, yr.)

27C. NUMBER OF TIMES YOU HAVE BEEN MARRIED (To include current marriage)

27D. NUMBER OF TIMES YOUR PRESENT SPOUSE HAS BEEN MARRIED (To include current marriage)

27E. IS YOUR SPOUSE ALSO A VETERAN? ☐ YES ☐ NO (If "Yes," complete Item 27F)

27F. SPOUSE'S VA FILE NUMBER (if any) C-

27G. DO YOU LIVE TOGETHER? ☐ YES ☐ NO (If "No," complete Items 27H thru 27I)

27H. REASON FOR SEPARATION (For example, marital problems, job requirements, health, etc.)

27I. PRESENT ADDRESS OF SPOUSE

27J. AMOUNT YOU CONTRIBUTE TO YOUR SPOUSE'S MONTHLY SUPPORT $

27K. HOW WERE YOU MARRIED? ☐ CLERGYMAN OR AUTHORIZED PUBLIC OFFICIAL ☐ COMMON-LAW ☐ TRIBAL ☐ PROXY ☐ OTHER (Explain)

YOU MUST SIGN AND PRINT YOUR NAME AND DATE THIS FORM IN ITEMS 42A THRU 42C ON PAGE 10.

Sample VA Form 21-526 (continued)

Go to www.va.gov\vaforms to download and print this form.

PART VIII - INCOME INFORMATION *(Provide the income you received from all sources)*

NOTE: Report the total income before deductions for taxes, insurance, etc. If you do not receive any payments from one of the sources that we list, write "0" or "None" in the space. If you are receiving monthly benefits, give us a copy of your most recent award letter. This will help us determine the amount of benefits you should be paid. Payments from any source will be counted, unless the law says that they don't need to be counted.

MONTHLY INCOME - Provide the income that you and your dependents receive every month. For items 35A -35F, if none, write "0" or "NONE." Do not leave blank spaces.

ITEM NO.	SOURCES OF RECURRING MONTHLY INCOME	VETERAN	SPOUSE	CHILD(REN) *(Provide the first, middle initial, and last name)*		
				NAME	NAME	NAME
35A.	Social Security					
35B.	U.S. Civil Service					
35C.	U.S. Railroad Retirement					
35D.	Military Retired Pay					
35E.	Black Lung Benefits					
35F.	Other *(Interest, dividends or one-time payments)*					

35A. WILL YOU RECEIVE ANY INCOME FROM RENTAL PROPERTY OR FROM THE OPERATION OF A BUSINESS WITHIN 12 MONTHS OF THE DAY YOU SIGN THIS FORM? ☐ YES ☐ NO	35B. WILL YOU RECEIVE ANY INCOME FROM THE OPERATION OF A FARM WITHIN 12 MONTHS OF THE DAY YOU SIGN THIS FORM? ☐ YES ☐ NO	35C. DO YOU THINK YOUR INCOME WILL CHANGE IN THE NEXT 12 MONTHS? *(If "Yes," explain below)* ☐ YES ☐ NO

PART IX - NET WORTH *(Provide specific information about the net worth of you and your dependents)*

NET WORTH is the market value of all interest and rights in any kind of property after subtracting any mortgages or other claims against the property. However, net worth does not include the house you live in or a reasonable area of land it sits on. Net worth also does not include the value of personal items such as your vehicle, clothing, and furniture.

NOTE: For items 37A-37F provide amounts. If none, write "0" OR "NONE." Do not leave blank spaces.

ITEM NO.	SOURCE	VETERAN	SPOUSE	CHILD(REN) *(Provide the first, middle initial, and last name)*		
				NAME	NAME	NAME
37A.	Cash, non-interest bearing bank accounts					
37B.	Interest bearing bank accounts, certificates of deposit (CDs)					
37C.	Retirement accounts (IRAs, Keogh Plans, etc.)					
37D.	Stocks, bonds, and mutual funds					
37E.	Value of business assets					
37F.	Real property (not your home)					

YOU MUST SIGN AND PRINT YOUR NAME AND DATE THIS FORM IN ITEMS 42A THRU 42C ON PAGE 19.

Sample VA Form 21-526b

Go to www.va.gov\vaforms to download and print this form.

Sample VA Form 21-0960E-1

Go to www.va.gov\vaforms to download and print this form.

OMB Control No. 2900-0776
Respondent Burden: 15 minutes

VA Department of Veterans Affairs	DIABETES MELLITUS DISABILITY BENEFITS QUESTIONNAIRE

IMPORTANT - THE DEPARTMENT OF VETERANS AFFAIRS (VA) WILL NOT PAY OR REIMBURSE ANY EXPENSES OR COST INCURRED IN THE PROCESS OF COMPLETING AND/OR SUBMITTING THIS FORM. PLEASE READ THE PRIVACY ACT AND RESPONDENT BURDEN INFORMATION BEFORE COMPLETING FORM.

NAME OF PATIENT/VETERAN	PATIENT/VETERAN'S SOCIAL SECURITY NUMBER

NOTE TO PHYSICIAN - Your patient is applying to the U.S. Department of Veterans Affairs (VA) for disability benefits. VA will consider the information you provide on this questionnaire as part of their evaluation in processing the veteran's claim.

SECTION I - DIAGNOSIS

1A. SELECT THE VETERAN'S CONDITION:

☐ DIABETES MELLITUS TYPE I
☐ DIABETES MELLITUS TYPE II
☐ IMPAIRED FASTING GLUCOSE
☐ DOES NOT MEET CRITERIA FOR DIAGNOSIS OF DIABETES
☐ OTHER (Specify, providing only diagnoses that pertain to Diabetes Mellitus or its complications)

DIAGNOSIS # 1 -	ICD CODE -	DATE OF DIAGNOSIS -
DIAGNOSIS # 2 -	ICD CODE -	DATE OF DIAGNOSIS -
DIAGNOSIS # 3 -	ICD CODE -	DATE OF DIAGNOSIS -

1B. IF THERE ARE ADDITIONAL DIAGNOSES THAT PERTAIN TO DIABETES MELLITUS LIST USING ABOVE FORMAT

SECTION II - MEDICAL HISTORY

2A. TREATMENT (Check all that apply):

☐ NONE
☐ MANAGED BY RESTRICTED DIET
☐ PRESCRIBED ORAL HYPOGLYCEMIC AGENT(S)
☐ PRESCRIBED INSULIN 1 INJECTION PER DAY
☐ PRESCRIBED INSULIN MORE THAN 1 INJECTION PER DAY
☐ OTHER (Describe)

2B. DOES THE VETERAN REQUIRE REGULATION OF ACTIVITIES AS PART OF MEDICAL MANAGEMENT OF DIABETES MELLITUS?

☐ YES   ☐ NO   (If "Yes," provide one or more examples of how the veteran must regulate his or her activities):

NOTE - For VA purposes, regulation of activities can be defined as avoidance of strenuous occupational and recreational activities with the intention of avoiding hypoglycemic episodes.

2C. HOW FREQUENTLY DOES THE VETERAN VISIT HIS OR HER DIABETIC CARE PROVIDER FOR EPISODES OF KETOACIDOSIS OR HYPOGLYCEMIC REACTIONS?

☐ LESS THAN 2 TIMES PER MONTH   ☐ 2 TIMES PER MONTH   ☐ WEEKLY

2D. HOW MANY EPISODES OF KETOACIDOSIS REQUIRING HOSPITALIZATION OVER THE PAST 12 MONTHS?

☐ 0   ☐ 1   ☐ 2   ☐ 3 OR MORE

2E. HOW MANY EPISODES OF HYPOGLYCEMIA REQUIRING HOSPITALIZATION OVER THE PAST 12 MONTHS?

☐ 0   ☐ 1   ☐ 2   ☐ 3 OR MORE

2F. HAS THE VETERAN HAD PROGRESSIVE UNINTENTIONAL WEIGHT LOSS ATTRIBUTABLE TO DIABETES MELLITUS?

☐ YES   ☐ NO   (If "Yes," provide percent of loss of individual's baseline weight): _____%

NOTE - For VA purposes, "baseline weight" means the average weight for the two-year period preceding the onset of the disease.

2G. HAS THE VETERAN HAD PROGRESSIVE LOSS OF STRENGTH ATTRIBUTABLE TO DIABETES MELLITUS?

☐ YES   ☐ NO

VA FORM
JAN 2011   **21-0960E-1**   Page 1

Sample VA Form 21-0960E-1 (continued)

Go to www.va.gov\vaforms to download and print this form.

Sample VA Form 21-0960E-1 (continued)

Go to www.va.gov\vaforms to download and print this form.

SECTION V - DIAGNOSTIC TESTING

5A. TEST RESULTS USED TO MAKE THE DIAGNOSIS OF DIABETES MELLITUS *(if known) (Check all that apply)*

NOTE: If laboratory test results are in the medical record, repeat testing is not required. A glucose tolerance test is not required for VA purposes, report this test only if already completed.

- [ ] FASTING PLASMA GLUCOSE TEST (FPG) OF ±126 MG/DL ON 2 OR MORE OCCASIONS *(Date)* _____
- [ ] A1C OF 6.5% OR GREATER ON 2 OR MORE OCCASIONS *(Date)* _____
- [ ] 2-HR PLASMA GLUCOSE OF ±200 MG/DL ON GLUCOSE TOLERANCE TEST *(Date)* _____
- [ ] RANDOM PLASMA GLUCOSE OF ±200 MG/DL WITH CLASSIC SYMPTOMS OF HYPERGLYCEMIA *(Date)* _____
- [ ] OTHER *(Describe):*

5B. CURRENT TEST RESULTS

MOST RECENT A1C, IF AVAILABLE _____ *(Date)* _____

MOST RECENT FASTING PLASMA GLUCOSE, IF AVAILABLE _____ *(Date)* _____

SECTION VI - FUNCTIONAL IMPACT

6. DOES THE VETERAN'S DIABETES MELLITUS CONDITION *(and complications of Diabetes Mellitus if present)* IMPACT HIS OR HER ABILITY TO WORK? *Impact on ability to work may also be addressed on the individual Questionnaire(s) for other diabetes-associated conditions and/or complications, if complaint)*

- [ ] YES [ ] NO *(If Yes," separately describe impact of each of the veteran's Diabetes Mellitus, diabetes-associated conditions, and complications, if present, providing one or more examples)*

SECTION VII - REMARKS

7. REMARKS *(if any)*

SECTION VIII - PHYSICIAN'S CERTIFICATION AND SIGNATURE

CERTIFICATION - To the best of my knowledge, the information contained herein is accurate, complete and current.

8A. PHYSICIAN'S SIGNATURE	8B. PHYSICIAN'S PRINTED NAME	8C. DATE SIGNED
8D. PHYSICIAN'S PHONE AND FAX NUMBERS	8E. PHYSICIAN'S MEDICAL LICENSE NUMBER	8F. PHYSICIAN'S ADDRESS

NOTE - VA may request additional medical information, including additional examinations, if necessary to complete VA's review of the veteran's application.

IMPORTANT - Physician please fax the completed form to _____

(VA Regional Office FAX No.)

NOTE - A list of VA Regional Office FAX Numbers can be found at www.vba.va.gov/disabilityexams or obtained by calling 1-800-827-1000.

PRIVACY ACT NOTICE: VA will not disclose information collected on this form to any source other than what has been authorized under the Privacy Act of 1974 or Title 38, Code of Federal Regulations 1.576 for routine uses (i.e., civil or criminal law enforcement, congressional communications, epidemiological or research studies, the collection of money owed to the United States, litigation in which the United States is a party or has an interest, the administration of VA programs and delivery of VA benefits, verification of identity and status, and personnel administration) as identified in the VA system of records, 58VA21/22/28, Compensation, Pension, Education and Vocational Rehabilitation and Employment Records - VA, published in the Federal Register. Your obligation to respond is voluntary. VA uses your SSN to identify your claim file. Providing your SSN will help ensure that your records are properly associated with your claim file. Giving us your SSN account information is voluntary. Refusal to provide your SSN by itself will not result in the denial of benefits. VA will not deny an individual benefits for refusing to provide his or her SSN unless the disclosure of the SSN is required by a Federal Statute of law in effect prior to January 1, 1975, and still in effect. The requested information is considered relevant and necessary to determine maximum benefits under the law. The responses you submit are considered confidential (38 U.S.C. 5701). Information submitted is subject to verification through computer matching programs with other agencies.

RESPONDENT BURDEN: We need this information to determine entitlement to benefits (38 U.S.C. 501). Title 38, United States Code, allows us to ask for this information. We estimate that you will need an average of 15 minutes to review the instructions, find the information, and complete this form. VA cannot conduct or sponsor a collection of information unless a valid OMB control number is displayed. You are not required to respond to a collection of information if this number is not displayed. Valid OMB control numbers can be located on the OMB Internet Page at www.reginfo.gov/public/do/PRAMain. If desired, you can call 1-800-827-1000 to get information on where to send comments or suggestions about this form.

118

Sample VA Form 21-2680

Go to www.va.gov\vaforms to download and print this form.

OMB Control No. 2900-0721
Respondent Burden: 30 minutes

Department of Veterans Affairs

EXAMINATION FOR HOUSEBOUND STATUS OR PERMANENT NEED FOR REGULAR AID AND ATTENDANCE

1. FIRST NAME - MIDDLE NAME - LAST NAME OF VETERAN	2. FIRST NAME - MIDDLE NAME - LAST NAME OF CLAIMANT (If other than veteran)	3. RELATIONSHIP OF CLAIMANT TO VETERAN

4A. VETERANS SOCIAL SECURITY NUMBER	4B. CLAIMANT'S SOCIAL SECURITY NUMBER	5. CLAIM NUMBER

6. DATE OF EXAMINATION	7. HOME ADDRESS

8A. IS CLAIMANT HOSPITALIZED?	8B. DATE ADMITTED	9. NAME AND ADDRESS OF HOSPITAL
☐ YES ☐ NO (If "Yes," complete items 8B and 9)		

NOTE: EXAMINER PLEASE READ CAREFULLY

The purpose of this examination is to record manifestations and findings pertinent to the question of whether the claimant is housebound (confined to the home or immediate premises) or is in need of the regular aid and attendance of another person.

The report should be in sufficient detail for the VA decision makers to determine the extent that disease or injury produces physical or mental impairment, that loss of coordination or enfeeblement affects the ability to dress and undress, to feed him/herself, to attend to the wants of nature, or keep him/herself ordinarily clean and presentable.

Findings should be recorded to show whether the claimant is blind or bedridden.

Whether the claimant seeks housebound or aid and attendance benefits, the report should reflect how well he/she ambulates, where he/she goes, and what he/she is able to do during a typical day.

10. COMPLETE DIAGNOSIS (Diagnosis needs to equate to the level of assistance described in questions 20 through 34)

11A. AGE	11B. SEX	12. WEIGHT		13. HEIGHT	
		ACTUAL: LBS ESTIMATED: LBS		FEET: INCHES:	

14. NUTRITION		15. GAIT

16. BLOOD PRESSURE	17. PULSE RATE	18. RESPIRATORY RATE	19. WHAT DISABILITIES RESTRICT THE LISTED ACTIVITIES/FUNCTIONS?

20. IF THE CLAIMANT IS CONFINED TO BED, INDICATE THE NUMBER OF HOURS IN BED

From 9 PM To 9 AM: From 9 AM To 9 PM:

21. IS THE CLAIMANT ABLE TO FEED HIM/HERSELF? (If "Yes," provide explanation)

☐ YES   ☐ NO

22. IS CLAIMANT ABLE TO PREPARE OWN MEALS? (If "Yes," provide explanation)

☐ YES   ☐ NO

23. DOES THE CLAIMANT NEED ASSISTANCE IN BATHING AND TENDING TO OTHER HYGIENE NEEDS? (If "Yes," provide explanation)

☐ YES   ☐ NO

24A. IS THE CLAIMANT LEGALLY BLIND? (If "Yes," provide explanation)	24B. CORRECTED VISION	
	LEFT EYE	RIGHT EYE
☐ YES ☐ NO		

25. DOES THE CLAIMANT REQUIRE NURSING HOME CARE? (If "Yes," provide explanation)

☐ YES   ☐ NO

26. DOES CLAIMANT REQUIRE MEDICATION MANAGEMENT? (If "Yes," provide explanation)

☐ YES   ☐ NO

27. DOES THE CLAIMANT HAVE THE ABILITY TO MANAGE HIS/HER OWN FINANCIAL AFFAIRS? (If "No," provide explanation)

☐ YES   ☐ NO

VA FORM JUN 2008   **21-2680**   SUPERSEDES VA FORM 21-2680, OCT 1992, WHICH WILL NOT BE USED.

Sample VA Form 21-2680 (continued)

Go to www.va.gov\vaforms to download and print this form.

28. POSTURE AND GENERAL APPEARANCE *(Attach a separate sheet of paper if additional space is needed)*

29. DESCRIBE RESTRICTIONS OF EACH UPPER EXTREMITY WITH PARTICULAR REFERENCE TO GRIP, FINE MOVEMENTS, AND ABILITY TO FEED HIM/HERSELF, TO BUTTON CLOTHING, SHAVE AND ATTEND TO THE NEEDS OF NATURE *(Attach a separate sheet of paper if additional space is needed)*

30. DESCRIBE RESTRICTIONS OF EACH LOWER EXTREMITY WITH PARTICULAR REFERENCE TO THE EXTENT OF LIMITATION OF MOTION, ATROPHY, AND CONTRACTURESSOR OTHER INTERFERENCE. IF INDICATED, COMMENT SPECIFICALLY ON WEIGHT BEARING, BALANCE AND PROPULSION OF EACH LOWER EXTREMITY.

31. DESCRIBE RESTRICTION OF THE SPINE, TRUNK AND NECK

32. SET FORTH ALL OTHER PATHOLOGY INCLUDING THE LOSS OF BOWEL OR BLADDER CONTROL OR THE EFFECTS OF ADVANCING AGE, SUCH AS DIZZINESS, LOSS OF MEMORY OR POOR BALANCE, THAT AFFECTS CLAIMANT'S ABILITY TO PERFORM SELF-CARE, AMBULATE OR TRAVEL BEYOND THE PREMISES OF THE HOME, OR, IF HOSPITALIZED, BEYOND THE WARD OR CLINICAL AREA. DESCRIBE WHERE THE CLAIMANT GOES AND WHAT HE OR SHE DOES DURING A TYPICAL DAY.

33. DESCRIBE HOW OFTEN PER DAY OR WEEK AND UNDER WHAT CIRCUMSTANCES THE CLAIMANT IS ABLE TO LEAVE THE HOME OR IMMEDIATE PREMISES

34. ARE AIDS SUCH AS CANES, BRACES, CRUTCHES, OR THE ASSISTANCE OF ANOTHER PERSON REQUIRED FOR LOCOMOTION? *(If so, specify and describe effectiveness in terms of distance that can be traveled, as in Item 32 above)*

☐ YES *(If "YES" give distance)/Check applicable box or specify distance)*   ☐ 1 BLOCK   ☐ 5 or 6 BLOCKS   ☐ 1 MILE   OTHER *(Specify distance)* _____
☐ NO

35A. PRINTED NAME OF EXAMINING PHYSICIAN	35B. SIGNATURE AND TITLE OF EXAMINING PHYSICIAN	35C. DATE SIGNED

36A. NAME AND ADDRESS OF MEDICAL FACILITY	36B. TELEPHONE NUMBER OF MEDICAL FACILITY *(Include Area Code)*

Sample VA Form 21-4138

Go to www.va.gov\vaforms to download and print this form.

STATEMENT IN SUPPORT OF CLAIM

VA FORM 21-4138

Sample VA Form 21-4142

Go to www.va.gov\vaforms to download and print this form.

Department of Veterans Affairs

AUTHORIZATION AND CONSENT TO RELEASE INFORMATION TO THE DEPARTMENT OF VETERANS AFFAIRS (VA)

RESPONDENT BURDEN: We need this information to obtain your treatment records. Title 38, United States Code, allows us to ask for this information. We estimate that you will need an average of 5 minutes to review the instructions, find the information and complete this form. VA cannot conduct or sponsor a collection of information unless a valid OMB control number is displayed. You are not required to respond to a collection of information if this number is not displayed. Valid OMB control numbers can be located on the OMB Internet Page at http://reginfo.gov/public/do/PRAMain. If desired, you can call 1-800-827-1000 to get information on where to send comments or suggestions about this form.

IF YOU HAVE ANY QUESTIONS ABOUT THIS FORM, CALL VA TOLL-FREE AT 1-800-827-1000 (TDD 1-800-829-4833 FOR HEARING IMPAIRED).

SECTION I - VETERAN/CLAIMANT IDENTIFICATION

1. LAST NAME - FIRST NAME - MIDDLE NAME OF VETERAN (Type or print)	2. VETERAN'S VA FILE NUMBER
3. CLAIMANT'S NAME (If other than Veteran) LAST NAME, FIRST, MIDDLE	4. VETERAN'S SOCIAL SECURITY NUMBER
5. RELATIONSHIP OF CLAIMANT TO VETERAN	6. CLAIMANT'S SOCIAL SECURITY NUMBER

SECTION II - SOURCE OF INFORMATION

7A. LIST THE NAME AND ADDRESS OF THE SOURCE SUCH AS A PHYSICIAN, HOSPITAL, ETC. (Include ZIP Codes, and also a telephone number, if available) NOTE: If the source is your physician please provide their first and last name.	7B. DATE(S) OF TREATMENT, HOSPITALIZATIONS, OFFICE VISITS, DISCHARGE FROM TREATMENT OR CARE, ETC. (Include month and year)	7C. CONDITION(S) (List illness, injury, etc. pertinent to your claim)

8. COMMENTS:

YOU MUST SIGN AND DATE THIS FORM ON PAGE 2 AND CHECK THE APPROPRIATE BLOCK IN ITEM 9C.

VA FORM JAN 2011 **21-4142** — Existing stocks of the VA Form 21-4142, Sep 2009, will be used. — PAGE 1

Sample VA Form 21-4142 (continued)

Go to www.va.gov\vaforms to download and print this form.

SECTION III - CONSENT TO RELEASE INFORMATION

READ ALL PARAGRAPHS CAREFULLY BEFORE SIGNING. YOU MUST CHECK THE APPROPRIATE STATEMENT UNDERLINED IN PARENTHESES IN PARAGRAPH 9C.

9A. **Privacy Act Notice:** The VA will not disclose information collected on this form to any source other than what has been authorized under the Privacy Act of 1974 or Title 38, Code of Federal Regulations 1.576 for routine uses (i.e., civil or criminal law enforcement, congressional communications, epidemiological or research studies, the collection of money owed to the United States, litigation in which the United States is a party or has an interest, the administration of VA programs and delivery of VA benefits, verification of identity and status, and personnel administration) as identified in the VA system of records, 58VA21/22/28 Compensation, Pension, Education, and Vocational Rehabilitation and Employment Records - VA, published in the Federal Register. Your obligation to respond is voluntary. However, if the information including your Social Security Number (SSN) is not furnished completely or accurately, the health care provider to which this authorization is addressed may not be able to identify and locate your records, and provide a copy to VA. VA uses your SSN to identify your claim file. Providing your SSN will help ensure that your records are properly associated with your claim file. Giving us your SSN account information is voluntary. Refusal to provide your SSN by itself will not result in the denial of benefits. The VA will not deny an individual benefits for refusing to provide his or her SSN unless the disclosure of the SSN is required by Federal Statute of law in effect prior to January 1, 1975, and still in effect.

9B. I, the undersigned, hereby authorize the hospital, physician or other health care provider or health plan shown in Item 7A to release any information that may have been obtained in connection with a physical, psychological or psychiatric examination or treatment, with the understanding that VA will use this information in determining my eligibility to veterans benefits I have claimed. I understand that the health care provider or health plan identified in Item 7A who is being asked to provide the Veterans Benefits Administration with records under this authorization may not require me to execute this authorization before it will, or will continue to, provide me with treatment, payment for health care, enrollment in a health plan, or eligibility for benefits provided by it. I understand that once my health care provider sends this information to VA under this authorization, the information will no longer be protected by the HIPAA Privacy Rule, but will be protected by the Federal Privacy Act, 5 USC 552a, and VA may disclose this information as authorized by law. I also understand that I may revoke this authorization, at anytime (except to the extent that the health care provider has already released information to VA under this authorization) by notifying the health care provider shown in Item 7A. Please contact the VA Regional Office handling your claim or the Board of Veterans' Appeals, if an appeal is pending, regarding such action. If you do not revoke this authorization, it will automatically end 180 days from the date you sign and date the form (Item 10C).

9C. I ☐ (AUTHORIZE) ☐ (DO NOT AUTHORIZE) the source shown in Item 7A to release or disclose any information or records relating to the diagnosis, treatment or other therapy for the condition(s) of drug abuse, alcoholism or alcohol abuse, infection with the human immunodeficiency virus (HIV), sickle cell anemia or psychotherapy notes. IF MY CONSENT TO THIS INFORMATION IS LIMITED, THE LIMITATION IS WRITTEN HERE:

10A. SIGNATURE OF VETERAN/CLAIMANT OR LEGAL REPRESENTATIVE	10B. RELATIONSHIP TO VETERAN/CLAIMANT *(If other than self, please provide full name, title, organization, city, State and ZIP Code. All court appointments must include docket number, county and State)*	10C. DATE
10D. MAILING ADDRESS *(Number and Street or rural route, city, or P.O. State and ZIP Code)*	10E. TELEPHONE NUMBER *(Include Area Code)*	

The signature and address of a person who either knows the person signing this form or is satisfied as to that person's identity is requested below. This is not required by VA but may be required by the source of the information.

11A. SIGNATURE OF WITNESS	11B. DATE
11C. MAILING ADDRESS OF WITNESS	

VA FORM 21-4142, JAN 2011

PAGE 2

Sample VA Form 21-0781a

Go to www.va.gov\vaforms to download and print this form.

OMB Approved No. 2900-6659
Respondent Burden: 1 hour 10 minutes

Department of Veterans Affairs

VA DATE STAMP
DO NOT WRITE IN THIS SPACE

STATEMENT IN SUPPORT OF CLAIM FOR SERVICE CONNECTION FOR POST-TRAUMATIC STRESS DISORDER (PTSD) SECONDARY TO PERSONAL ASSAULT

INSTRUCTIONS: List the stressful incident or incidents that occurred in service that you feel contributed to your current condition. For each incident, provide a description of what happened, the date, the geographic location, your unit assignment and dates of assignment. Please complete the form in detail and be as specific as possible so that research of military records and other sources you identify can be thoroughly conducted. If more space is needed, attach a separate sheet, indicating the item number to which the answers apply.

1. NAME OF VETERAN *(First, Middle, Last)*

2. VA FILE NO.

STRESSFUL INCIDENT NO. 1

3A. DATE INCIDENT OCCURRED *(Mo., day, yr.)*

3B. LOCATION OF INCIDENT *(City, State, Country, Province, landmark or military installation)*

3C. UNIT ASSIGNMENT DURING INCIDENT *(Such as, DIVISION, WING, BATTALION, CAVALRY, SHIP)*

3D. DATES OF UNIT ASSIGNMENT *(Mo., day, yr.)*
FROM
TO

3E. DESCRIPTION OF THE INCIDENT

4. OTHER SOURCES OF INFORMATION: Identify any other sources (military or non-military) that may provide information concerning the incident. If you reported the incident to military or civilian authorities or sought help from a rape crisis center, counseling facility, or health clinic, etc., please provide the names and addresses and we will assist you in getting the information. If the source provided treatment and you would like us to obtain the treatment records, complete VA Form 21-4142, Authorization and Consent to Release Information to the Department of Veterans Affairs (VA), for each provider. If you confided in roommates, family members, chaplains, clergy, or fellow service persons, you may want to ask them for a statement concerning their knowledge of the incident. These statements will help us in deciding your claim. Other sources of information also include personal diaries or journals.

NAME	ADDRESS
NAME	ADDRESS
NAME	ADDRESS

VA FORM
OCT 2007 **21-0781a**

EXISTING STOCK OF VA FORM 21-0781A, JUL 2004, WILL BE USED.

124

Sample VA Form 21-0781a (continued)

Go to www.va.gov\vaforms to download and print this form.

STRESSFUL INCIDENT NO. 2

5A. DATE INCIDENT OCCURRED (Mo., day, yr.)	5B. LOCATION OF INCIDENT (City, State, Country, Province, landmark or military installation)

5C. UNIT ASSIGNMENT DURING INCIDENT (Such as, DIVISION, WING, BATTALION, CAVALRY, SHIP)	5D. DATES OF UNIT ASSIGNMENT (Mo., day, yr.)
	FROM / TO

5E. DESCRIPTION OF THE INCIDENT

6. OTHER SOURCES OF INFORMATION: Identify any other sources (military or non-military) that may provide information concerning the incident. If you reported the incident to military or civilian authorities or sought help from a rape crisis center, counseling facility, or health clinic, etc., please provide the names and addresses and we will assist you in getting the information. If the source provided treatment and you would like us to obtain the treatment records, complete VA Form 21-4142, Authorization and Consent to Release Information to the Department of Veterans Affairs (VA), for each provider. If you confided in roommates, family members, chaplains, clergy, or fellow service persons, you may want to ask them for a statement concerning their knowledge of the incident. These statements will help us in deciding your claim. Other sources of information also include personal diaries or journals.

NAME	ADDRESS
NAME	ADDRESS
NAME	ADDRESS

VA FORM 21-0781a, OCT 2007

Sample VA Form 21-0781a (continued)

Go to www.va.gov\vaforms to download and print this form.

7. Please provide in the space below any other information that you feel is important for us to know that may help your claim. Let us know if you experienced any of the following or other behavior changes following the incident(s):

- visits to a medical or counseling clinic or dispensary without a specific diagnosis or specific ailment
- sudden requests for a change in occupational series or duty assignment
- increased use of leave without an apparent reason
- changes in performance and performance evaluations
- episodes of depression, panic attacks, or anxiety without an identifiable cause
- increased or decreased use of prescription medications
- increased use of over-the-counter medications

- substance abuse such as alcohol or drugs
- increased disregard for military or civilian authority
- obsessive behavior such as overeating or undereating
- pregnancy tests around the time of the incident
- tests for HIV or sexually transmitted diseases
- unexplained economic or social behavior changes
- breakup of a primary relationship

I CERTIFY THAT the foregoing statement(s) are true and correct to the best of my knowledge and belief.

8. SIGNATURE	9. DATE	10. TELEPHONE NUMBERS *(Include Area Code)*	
		DAYTIME	EVENING

PENALTY - The law provides severe penalties which include fine or imprisonment or both, for the willful submission of any statement or evidence of a material fact, knowing it is false, or fraudulent acceptance of any payment to which you are not entitled.

PRIVACY ACT NOTICE: The VA will not disclose information collected on this form to any source other than what has been authorized under the Privacy Act of 1974 or Title 38, Code of Federal Regulations 1.576 for routine uses (i.e., civil or criminal law enforcement, congressional communications, epidemiological or research studies, the collection of money owed to the United States, litigation in which the United States is a party or has an interest, the administration of VA programs and delivery of VA benefits, verification of identity and status, and personnel administration) as identified in the VA system of records, 58VA21/22. Compensation, Pension, Education and Rehabilitation Records - VA, published in the Federal Register. Your obligation to respond is voluntary. However, the requested information is necessary to obtain supporting evidence of stressful incidents in service. If the information is not furnished completely or accurately, VA will not be able to thoroughly research your military records and other sources for supporting evidence. The responses you submit are considered confidential (38 U.S.C. 5701).

RESPONDENT BURDEN: We need this information in order to assist you in supporting your claim for post-traumatic stress disorder (38 U.S.C. 5107 (a)). Title 38, United States Code, allows us to ask for this information. We estimate that you will need an average of 1 hour and 10 minutes to review the instructions, find the information, and complete this form. VA cannot conduct or sponsor a collection of information unless a valid OMB control number is displayed. You are not required to respond to a collection of information if this number is not displayed. Valid OMB control numbers can be located on the OMB Internet Page at www.whitehouse.gov/omb/library/OMBINV.VA.EPA.html#VA. If desired, you can call 1-800-827-1000 to get information on where to send comments or suggestions about this form.

VA FORM 21-0781a, OCT 2007

A Guide to Obtaining Veterans Administration Compensation Benefits

Sample VA Form 21-0781

Go to www.va.gov\vaforms to download and print this form.

Sample VA Form 21-0781 (continued)

Go to www.va.gov\vaforms to download and print this form.

STRESSFUL INCIDENT NO. 2

6A. DATE INCIDENT OCCURRED *(Mo., day, yr.)*	6B. LOCATION OF INCIDENT *(City, State, Country, Province, landmark or military installation)*	

6C. UNIT ASSIGNMENT DURING INCIDENT *(Such as, DIVISION, WING, BATTALION, CAVALRY, SHIP)*	6D. DATES OF UNIT ASSIGNMENT *(Mo., day, yr.)*	
	FROM	TO

6E. DESCRIPTION OF THE INCIDENT

6F. MEDALS OR CITATIONS YOU RECEIVED BECAUSE OF THE INCIDENT

INFORMATION ABOUT SERVICEPERSONS WHO WERE KILLED OR INJURED DURING INCIDENT NO. 2
(ATTACH A SEPARATE SHEET IF MORE SPACE IS NEEDED)

7A. NAME OF SERVICEPERSON *(First, Middle, Last)*	7B. RANK	7C. DATE OF INJURY/DEATH *(Mo. day, yr.)*

7D. PLEASE CHECK ONE	7E. UNIT ASSIGNMENT DURING INCIDENT *(Such as, DIVISION, WING, BATTALION, CAVALRY, SHIP)*
☐ KILLED IN ACTION ☐ WOUNDED IN ACTION ☐ KILLED NON-BATTLE ☐ INJURED NON-BATTLE	

8A. NAME OF SERVICEPERSON *(First, Middle, Last)*	8B. RANK	8C. DATE OF INJURY/DEATH *(Mo. day, yr.)*

8D. PLEASE CHECK ONE	8E. UNIT ASSIGNMENT DURING INCIDENT *(Such as, DIVISION, WING, BATTALION, CAVALRY, SHIP)*
☐ KILLED IN ACTION ☐ WOUNDED IN ACTION ☐ KILLED NON-BATTLE ☐ INJURED NON-BATTLE	

9. REMARKS

I certify that the foregoing statement(s) are true and correct to the best of my knowledge and belief.

10. SIGNATURE	11. DATE	12. TELEPHONE NUMBERS *(Include Area Code)*	
		DAYTIME	EVENING

PENALTY - The law provides severe penalties which include fine or imprisonment or both, for the willful submission of any statement or evidence of a material fact, knowing it is false, or fraudulent acceptance of any payment to which you are not entitled.

PRIVACY ACT NOTICE. The VA will not disclose information collected on this form to any source other than what has been authorized under the Privacy Act of 1974 or Title 38, Code of Federal Regulations 1.576 for routine uses (i.e., civil or criminal law enforcement, congressional communications, epidemiological or research studies, the collection of money owed to the United States, litigation in which the United States is a party or has an interest, the administration of VA programs and delivery of VA benefits, verification of identity and status, and personnel administration) as identified in the VA system of records, 58VA21/22, Compensation, Pension, Education and Rehabilitation Records - VA, published in the Federal Register. Your obligation to respond is voluntary. However, the requested information is necessary to obtain supporting evidence of stressful incidents in service. If the information is not furnished completely or accurately, VA will not be able to thoroughly research your military records for supporting evidence. The responses you submit are considered confidential (38 U.S.C. 5701).

RESPONDENT BURDEN: We need this information in order to assist you in supporting your claim for post-traumatic stress disorder (38 U.S.C. 5107 (a)). Title 38, United States Code, allows us to ask for this information. We estimate that you will need an average of 1 hour 10 minutes to review the instructions, find the information, and complete this form. VA cannot conduct or sponsor a collection of information unless a valid OMB control number is displayed. You are not required to respond to a collection of information if this number is not displayed. Valid OMB control numbers can be located on the OMB Internet Page at www.whitehouse.gov/omb/library/OMBINV.VA.EPA.html#VA. If desired, you can call 1-800-827-1000 to get information on where to send comments or suggestions about this form.

Sample VA Form 21-534

Go to www.va.gov\vaforms to download and print this form.

Department of Veterans Affairs

Application for Dependency and Indemnity Compensation, Death Pension and Accrued Benefits by a Surviving Spouse or Child (Including Death Compensation if Applicable)
VA Form 21-534

OMB Approved No. 2900-0004
Respondent Burden: 1 hour 15 minutes

VA DATE STAMP
(DO NOT WRITE IN THIS SPACE)

Please read the attached "General Instructions" before you fill out this form.

SECTION I

Tell us what you are applying for and what you and the deceased veteran have applied for

1. Did the veteran ever file a claim with VA?
   ☐ YES ☐ NO   *(If "Yes," answer Item 2)*

2. What is the VA file number?

3. Has the surviving spouse or child ever filed a claim with VA?
   ☐ YES ☐ NO   *(If "Yes," answer Items 4 through 6)*

4. What is the VA file number?

5. What is the name of the person on whose service the claim was filed?

   First   Middle   Last

6. What is your relationship to that person?

7. Are you claiming service connection for cause of death?
   ☐ YES ☐ NO

SECTION II

Tell us about you and the deceased veteran

Attach a copy of the death certificate unless the veteran died in active service of the Army, Navy, Air Force, Marine Corps, or Coast Guard, or in a U.S. government institution.

8. What is the veteran's name?

   First   Middle   Last   Suffix *(If applicable)*

9. What is the veteran's Social Security number?

10a. Did the veteran serve under another name?
   ☐ YES ☐ NO
   (If "Yes," answer Item 10b)

10b. Please list the other name(s) the veteran served under.

11. What is the veteran's date of birth?

   mo. day yr.

12. What is the veteran's date of death?

   mo. day yr.

13. Was the veteran a former prisoner of war?
   ☐ YES ☐ NO

14. What is your name? *(First, Middle, Last Name)*

15. What is your relationship to the veteran? *(check one)*
   ☐ Surviving Spouse ☐ Child

16. What is your address?

   Street address, Rural Route, or P.O. Box   Apt. number

   City   State   ZIP Code   Country

17. What are your telephone numbers? *(Include Area Code)*

   Daytime
   Evening

18. What is your e-mail address?

19. What is your Social Security number?

20. What is your date of birth?

   mo. day yr.

VA FORM
MAR 2009   **21-534**   SUPERSEDES VA FORM 21-534, JUN 1993,
WHICH WILL NOT BE USED.

Sample VA Form 21-534 (continued)

Go to www.va.gov\vaforms to download and print this form.

SECTION III	Note: Skip to Section IV if the veteran was receiving VA compensation or pension at the time of his/her death.				
Tell us about the veteran's active duty service 1. Enter complete information for all periods of service. If more space is needed use Item 48 "Remarks." 2. If the veteran never filed a claim with VA, attach the original DD214 or a certified copy for each period of service listed. We will return original documents to you	21a. Entered Active Service *(first period)* mo. day yr.	21b. Place	21c. Service Number		
	21d. Left This Active Service mo. day yr.	21e. Place	21f. Branch of Service	21g. Grade, Rank or Rating	
	21h. Entered Active Service *(second period)* mo. day yr.	21i. Place	21j. Service Number		
	21k. Left This Active Service mo. day yr.	21l. Place	21m. Branch of Service	21n. Grade, Rank or Rating	

SECTION IV	You must furnish complete information about all marriages of the surviving spouse and the veteran. If you need additional space, please attach a separate sheet of paper providing the requested information.
Tell us about your and the veteran's marriages *Attach a copy of your marriage certificate showing your marriage to the veteran*	If you are claiming benefits as the surviving spouse of the veteran you should complete Items 22a through 27. If you are not the surviving spouse, skip to Section V.

The veteran's marriages

22a. How many times was the veteran married? _____

22b. Date of Marriage *(month, day, year)*	22c. Place *(city/state or country)*	22d. To whom married *(first, middle initial, last name)*	22e. Type of marriage *(ceremonial, common-law, proxy, tribal or other)*	22f. Date marriage ended *(month, day, year)*	22g. Place *(city/state or country)*	22h. How marriage ended *(death, divorce)*

22i. If you indicated "other" as type of marriage, please explain. _____

22j. At the time of your marriage to the veteran, were you aware of any reason the marriage might not be legally valid?

☐ YES ☐ NO   If you answered "Yes," please explain. _____

23a. How many times were you married? _____   23b. Have you remarried since the death of the veteran? ☐ YES ☐ NO

23c. Date of Marriage *(month, day, year)*	23d. Place *(city/state or country)*	23e. To whom married *(first, middle initial, last name)*	23f. Type of marriage *(ceremonial, common-law, proxy, tribal or other)*	23g. Date marriage ended *(month, day, year)*	23h. Place *(city/state or country)*	23i. How marriage ended *(death, divorce)*

23j. If you indicated "other" as type of marriage, please explain. _____

Sample VA Form 21-534 (continued)

Go to www.va.gov\vaforms to download and print this form.

SECTION IV Tell us about your and the veteran's marital history (continued)

| Answer Item 24 only if you were married to the veteran for less than one year. | 24. Was a child born to you and the veteran during your marriage or prior to your marriage? ☐ YES ☐ NO | 25. Are you expecting the birth of a child of the veteran? ☐ YES ☐ NO |
| | 26. Did you live continuously with the veteran from the date of marriage to the date of his/her death? ☐ YES ☐ NO *(If "No", answer Item 27)* | 27. What was the cause of the separation? Give the reason, date(s), and duration of the separation. If the separation was by court order, attach a copy of the order. |

SECTION V

Tell us about the unmarried children of the veteran

Note: You should provide a copy of the public record of birth or a copy of the court record of adoption for each child listed in Item 28a unless the veteran was receiving additional VA benefits for the child.

If you need additional space, please attach a separate sheet of paper providing the requested information about each child

Note: Skip to Section VI if you are not claiming benefits for any children that meet the following criteria.

VA recognizes the veteran's biological children, adopted children, and stepchildren as dependents. These children must be unmarried and:

- under age 18, or
- at least 18 but under 23 and pursuing an approved course of education, or
- of any age if they became permanently unable to support themselves before reaching age 18.

"Seriously disabled" (Item 29e) means that the child became permanently unable to support himself/herself before reaching age 18. Furnish a statement from an attending physician or other medical evidence which shows the nature and extent of the physical or mental impairment.

Note to surviving spouse: If entitlement to DIC is established, a "seriously disabled" child over age 18 is entitled to receive DIC benefits in his or her own right. A veteran's child who is seriously disabled and over age 18 must submit a separate VA Form 21-534 to apply for benefits

28a. Name of child (First, middle initial, last)	28b. Date and place of birth (City/State or Country)	28c. Social Security Number	29a. Biological	29b. Adopted	29c. Stepchild	29d. 18 - 23 yrs. old and in school	29e. Seriously disabled	29f. Child previously married
	mo. day yr.		☐	☐	☐	☐	☐	☐
	mo. day yr.		☐	☐	☐	☐	☐	☐
	mo. day yr.		☐	☐	☐	☐	☐	☐

VA FORM 21-534, MAR 2009

Sample VA Form 21-534 (continued)

Go to www.va.gov\vaforms to download and print this form.

SECTION V Tell us about the unmarried children of the veteran (continued)

Tell us about the children listed above that don't live with you.

30a. Name of child (first, middle initial, last)	30b. Child's Complete Address	30c. Name of person the child lives with (if applicable)	30d. Monthly amount you contribute to child's support
			$
			$
			$
			$

SECTION VI	31. Are you claiming aid and attendance allowance and/or housebound benefits because you need the regular assistance of another person, are having severe visual problems, or are housebound?	32a. Are you now in a nursing home?
Tell us if you are housebound, in a nursing home or require aid and attendance If you answered "yes" to Item 31 and are not in a nursing home, submit a statement from your doctor showing the extent of your disabilities. If you are in a nursing home, attach a statement signed by an official of the nursing home showing the date you were admitted to the nursing home, the level of care you receive, the amount you pay out-of-pocket for your care, and whether Medicaid covers all or part of your nursing home costs.	☐ YES ☐ NO (If "No," skip to section VII)	☐ YES ☐ NO (If "Yes," answer Items 32b and 32c also)
	32b. What is the name and complete mailing address of the facility?	32c. Does Medicaid cover all or part of your nursing home costs? ☐ YES ☐ NO (If "No," answer Item 32d also)
	32d. Have you applied for Medicaid? ☐ YES ☐ NO	

Sample VA Form 21-534 (continued)

Go to www.va.gov\vaforms to download and print this form.

SECTION VII

Tell us the net worth of you and your dependents

Note: If you are filing this application on behalf of a minor or incompetent child of the veteran and you are the child's custodian, you must report your net worth as well as the net worth of the child for whom benefits are claimed.

VA cannot pay you pension if your net worth is sizeable. Net worth is the market value of all interest and rights you have in any kind of property less any mortgages or other claims against the property. However, net worth does not include the house you live in or a reasonable area of land it sits on. Net worth also does not include the value of personal things you use everyday like your vehicle, clothing, and furniture. You must report net worth for yourself and all persons for whom you are claiming benefits.

For Items 33a through 33f, provide the amounts. If none, write "0" or "None."

Source	Surviving spouse or Custodian of children	Child(ren)		
		Name: *(first, middle initial, last)*	Name: *(first, middle initial, last)*	Name: *(first, middle initial, last)*
33a. Cash, bank accounts, certificates of deposit (CDs)				
33b. IRAs, Keogh Plans, etc.				
33c. Stocks, bonds, mutual funds				
33d. Value of business assets				
33e. Real property *(not your home)*				
33f. All other property				

SECTION VIII

Tell us about the income of you and your dependents

Payments from any source will be counted, unless the law says that they don't need to be counted. Report all income, and VA will determine any amount that does not count.

Note: If you are filing this application on behalf of a minor of whom you are the custodian, you must report your income as well as the income of each child for whom benefits are claimed.

Report the total amounts before you take out deductions for taxes, insurance, etc. Do not report the same information in both tables.

If you expect to receive a payment, but you don't know how much it will be, write "Unknown" in the space.

If you do not receive any payments from one of the sources that we list, write "0" or "None" in the space.

If you are receiving monthly benefits, give us a copy of your most recent award letter. This will help us determine the amount of benefits you should be paid.

34a. Have you claimed or are you receiving benefits from the Social Security Administration on your own behalf or on behalf of child(ren) in your custody? ☐ YES ☐ NO *(If "Yes," answer item 34b)*	34b. Is Social Security based on your own employment? ☐ YES ☐ NO
35. Has a surviving spouse or child filed a claim for compensation from the Office of Worker's Compensation Programs based on the death of the veteran? ☐ YES ☐ NO	36. Has a court awarded damages based on the death of the veteran or is a claim or legal action for damages pending? ☐ YES ☐ NO

37. Have you claimed or are you receiving Survivor Benefit Plan (SBP) annuity from a service department based on the death of the veteran? ☐ YES ☐ NO

Sample VA Form 21-534 (continued)

Go to www.va.gov\vaforms to download and print this form.

SECTION VIII Tell us about the income of you and your dependents (continued)

Monthly Income - Tell us the income you and your dependents receive every month

Source	Surviving spouse or Custodian of children	Child(ren)		
		Name: *(first, middle initial, last)*	Name: *(first, middle initial, last)*	Name: *(first, middle initial, last)*
38a. Social Security				
38b. U.S. Civil Service				
38c. U.S. Railroad Retirement				
38d. Military Retirement				
38e. Black Lung Benefits				
38f. Supplemental Security Income (SSI)/ Public Assistance				
38g. Other income received monthly *(Please write source below)*				

Expected income next 12 months - Tell us about other income for you and your dependents

Report expected income for the 12 month period following the veteran's death. If the claim is filed more than one year after the veteran died, report the expected income for the 12 month period from the date you sign this application.

Sources of income for the next 12 months	Surviving spouse or Custodian of children	Child(ren)		
		Name: *(first, middle initial, last)*	Name: *(first, middle initial, last)*	Name: *(first, middle initial, last)*
39a. Gross wages and salary				
39b. Total dividends and interest				
39c. Other income expected *(Please write source below)*				
39d. Other income expected *(Please write source below)*				

134

Sample VA Form 21-534 (continued)

Go to www.va.gov\vaforms to download and print this form.

SECTION IX	Family medical expenses and certain other expenses actually paid by you may be deductible from your income. Show the amount of any continuing family medical expenses such as the monthly Medicare deduction or nursing home costs you pay. Also, show unreimbursed last illness and burial expenses and educational or vocational rehabilitation expenses you paid. Last illness and burial expenses are unreimbursed amounts paid by you for the veteran's or his/her child's last illness and burial and the veteran's just debts. Educational or vocational rehabilitation expenses are amounts paid for courses of education, including tuition, fees, and materials. Do not include any expenses for which you were reimbursed. If you receive reimbursement after you have filed this claim, promptly advise the VA office handling your claim. If more space is needed attach a separate sheet.
Tell us about medical, last illness, burial or other unreimbursed expenses	

40a. Amount paid by you	40b. Date Paid	40c. Purpose (Medicare deduction, nursing home costs, burial expenses, etc.)	40d. Paid to (Name of nursing home, hospital, funeral home, etc.)	40e. Relationship of person for whom expenses paid
$	mo day yr			
$	mo day yr			
$	mo day yr			
$	mo day yr			

SECTION X	All Federal payments beginning January 2, 1999, must be made by electronic funds transfer (EFT) also called Direct Deposit. Please attach a voided personal check or deposit slip or provide the information requested below in Items 41, 42, and 43 to enroll in Direct Deposit. If you do not have a bank account we will give you a waiver from Direct Deposit, just check the box below in Item 41. The Treasury Department is working on making bank accounts available to you. Once these accounts are available, you will be able to decide whether you wish to sign-up for one of the accounts or continue to receive a paper check. You can also request a waiver if you have other circumstances that you feel would cause you a hardship to be enrolled in Direct Deposit. You can write to: Department of Veterans Affairs, 125 S. Main Street Suite B, Muskogee OK 74401-7004, and give us a brief description of why you do not wish to participate in Direct Deposit.
Give us direct deposit information	
If benefits are awarded we will need more information in order to process any payments to you. Please read the paragraph starting with "All Federal payments..." and then either:	41. Account number (Please check the appropriate box and provide that account number, if applicable) ☐ Checking ☐ I certify that I do not have an account with a financial institution or certified payment agent ☐ Savings Account number _____
1. Attach a voided check, or	42. Name of financial institution _____
2. Answer questions 41-43 to the right.	43. Routing or transit number _____

135

Sample VA Form 21-534 (continued)

Go to www.va.gov\vaforms to download and print this form.

SECTION XI	I certify and authorize the release of information:
Give us your signature	I certify that the statements in this document are true and complete to the best of my knowledge. I authorize any person or entity, including but not limited to any organization, service provider, employer, or government agency, to give the Department of Veterans Affairs any information about me except protected health information, and I waive any privilege which makes the information confidential

1. Read the box that starts, "I certify and authorize the release of information:"

44. Your signature	45. Today's date

2. Sign the box that says, "Your signature."

46a. Signature of witness (if claimant signed above using an "X")	46b. Printed name and address of witness

3. If you sign with an "X," then you must have 2 people you know witness you as you sign. They must then sign the form and post their names and addresses also.

47a. Signature of witness (if claimant signed above using an "X")	47b. Printed name and address of witness

SECTION XII

48. Remarks (if you need more space to answer a question or have a comment about a specific item number on this form please identify your answer or statement by the part and item number)

Remarks - Use this space for any additional statements that you would like to make concerning your application.

IMPORTANT

Penalty: The law provides severe penalties which include fine or imprisonment, or both, for the willful submission of any statement or evidence of a material fact, knowing it to be false, or for the fraudulent acceptance of any payment which you are not entitled to.

New VA Forms

In an effort to assist veterans and medical professionals in providing the precise information that the VA will require to grant a benefit, an entire group of forms has been created. These forms are all designated 21-0960 and have alpha-numeric designators assigned to them. These forms are printable, and fillable and can all be obtained through the local service officer or found at www.va.gov\vaforms. The form must be filled out by the medical professional, not the veteran! After obtaining the completed form, the veteran should then submit it to the VA as evidence, either directly to the local service officer, the appropriate regional office, or through their chosen service organization.

The complete list of forms and the conditions they deal with are as follows. The veteran should pay close attention to the wording of the form as some may deal with a specific affliction, and others are generic in nature (i.e. ischemic heart disease is 21-0960A-1 with the general heart condition being 21-0960A-4). For any confusion with the needed form, the veteran should contact his local service officer, the service organization who represents the veteran, or the VA at 1-800-827-1000 (nationwide).

21-0960C-10 Peripheral Nerves Conditions (Not Including Diabetic Sensory-Motor Peripheral Neuropathy) Disability Benefits Questionnaire
21-0960J-1 Kidney Conditions (Nephrology) Disability Benefits Questionnaire
21-0960C-8 Headaches (Including Migraine Headaches) Disability Benefits Questionnaire
21-0960G-2 Gallbladder and Pancreas Conditions Disability Benefits Questionnaire
21-0960K-2 Gynecological Conditions Disability Benefits Questionnaire
21-0960C-4 Diabetic Sensory-Motor Peripheral Neuropathy Disability Benefits Questionnaire
21-0960C-9 Multiple Sclerosis (MS) Disability Benefits Questionnaire
21-0960E-1 Diabetes Mellitus Disability Benefits Questionnaire
21-0960G-1 Esophageal Conditions (Including gastroesophageal reflux disease (GERD), hiatal hernia and other esophageal disorders) Disability Benefits Questionnaire
21-0960P-2 Mental Disorders (Other Than PTSD and Eating Disorders) Disability Benefits Questionnaire
21-0960A-3 Hypertension Disability Benefits Questionnaire

21-0960B-2 Hematologic and Lymphatic Conditions, Including Leukemia Disability Benefits Questionnaire
21-0960J-3 Prostate Cancer Disability Benefits Questionnaire
21-0960M-9 Knee and Lower Leg Conditions Disability Benefits Questionnaire
21-0960N-2 Eye Conditions Disability Benefits Questionnaire
21-0960A-4 Heart Conditions (Including Ischemic and Non-Ischemic Heart Disease, Arrhythmias, Valvular Disease and Cardiac Surgery) Disability Benefits Questionnaire
21-0960G-8 Infectious Intestinal Disorders, Including Bacterial and Parasitic Infections Disability Benefits Questionnaire
21-0960J-2 Male Reproductive Organ Conditions Disability Benefits Questionnaire
21-0960A-1 Ischemic Heart Disease (IHD) Disability Benefits Questionnaire
21-0960B-1 Hairy Cell and Other B-Cell Leukemias Disability Benefits Questionnaire
21-0960C-1 Parkinson's Disease Disability Benefits Questionnaire
21-0960M-15 Temporomandibular Joint (TMJ) Conditions Disability Benefits Questionnaire
21-0960D-1 Oral and Dental Conditions Including Mouth, Lips and Tongue (Other Than Temporomandibular Joint Conditions) Disability Benefits Questionnaire
21-0960N-4 Sinusitis/Rhinitis and Other Conditions of the Nose, Throat, Larynx and Pharynx Disability Benefits Questionnaire
21-0960L-1 Respiratory Conditions (Other than Tuberculosis and Sleep Apnea) Disability Benefits Questionnaire
21-0960I-2 HIV - Related Illnesses Disability Benefits Questionnaire
21-0960I-4 Systemic Lupus Erythematosus (SLE) and Other Autoimmune Diseases Disability Benefits Questionnaire
21-0960I-5 Nutritional Deficiencies Disability Benefits Questionnaire
21-0960C-3 Cranial Nerve Conditions Disability Benefits Questionnaire
21-0960C-6 Narcolepsy Disability Benefits Questionnaire
21-0960C-7 Fibromyalgia Disability Benefits Questionnaire
21-0960P-3 Review Post Traumatic Stress Disorder (PTSD) Disability Benefits Questionnaire
21-0960E-2 Endocrine Diseases (Other than Thyroid, Parathyroid or Diabetes Mellitus) Disability Benefits Questionnaire
21-0960E-3 Thyroid and Parathyroid Conditions Disability Benefits Questionnaire
21-0960M-11 Osteomyelitis Disability Benefits Questionnaire
21-0960M-13 Neck (Cervical Spine) Disability Benefits Questionnaire

21-0960P-1 Eating Disorders Disability Benefits Questionnaire
21-0960C-5 Central Nervous System and Neuromuscular Diseases (Except Trau. Brain Injury, etc.) Disability Benefits Questionnaire
21-0960M-4 Elbow and Forearm Conditions Disability Benefits Questionnaire
21-0960M-6 Foot Miscellaneous (Other Than Flatfoot/PES Planus) Disability Benefits Questionnaire
21-0960M-2 Ankle Conditions Disability Benefits Questionnaire
21-0960M-14 Back (Thoracolumbar Spine) Conditions Disability Benefits Questionnaire
21-0960N-1 Ear Conditions (Including Vestibular and Infectious Conditions) Disability Benefits Questionnaire
21-0960G-5 Hepatitis, Cirrhosis and Other Liver Conditions Disability Benefits Questionnaire
21-0960G-6 Peritoneal Adhesions Disability Benefits Questionnaire
21-0960I-6 Tuberculosis Disability Benefits Questionnaire
21-0960G-4 Intestinal Surgery (Bowel Resection, Colostomy, Ileostomy) Disability Benefits Questionnaire
21-0960K-1 Breast Conditions and Disorders Disability Benefits Questionnaire
21-0960N-3 Loss of Sense of Smell and/or Taste Disability Benefits Questionnaire
21-0960A-2 Artery and Vein Conditions (Vascular Diseases Including Varicose Veins) Disability Benefits Questionnaire
21-0960C-2 Amyotrophic Lateral Sclerosis (Lou Gehrig's Disease) Disability Benefits Questionnaire
21-0960J-4 Urinary Tract (Including Bladder and Urethra) Conditions (Excluding Male Reproductive System) Disability Benefits Questionnaire
21-0960H-1 Hernias (Including Abdominal, Inguinal and Femoral Hernias) Disability Benefits Questionnaire
21-0960I-3 Infectious Diseases (Other than HIV-Related Illness, Chronic Fatigue Syndrome, or Tuberculosis) Disability Benefits Questionnaire
21-0960M-7 Hand and Finger Conditions Disability Benefits Questionnaire
21-0960M-8 Hip and Thigh Conditions Disability Benefits Questionnaire
21-0960M-10 Muscle Injuries Disability Benefits Questionnaire
21-0960C-11 Seizure Disorders (Epilepsy) Disability Benefits Questionnaire
21-0960L-2 Sleep Apnea Disability Benefits Questionnaire
21-0960M-1 Amputations Disability Benefits Questionnaire

21-0960M-3 Non-Degenerative Arthritis (Including Inflammatory, Autoimmune, Crystalline and Infectious Arthritis) and Dysbaric Osteonecrosis Disability Benefits Questionnaire
21-0960G-7 Stomach and Duodenal Conditions (Not Including Gerd or Esophageal Disorders) Benefits Questionnaire
21-0960H-2 Rectum and Anus Conditions (Including Hemorrhoids) Benefits Questionnaire
21-0960I-1 Persian Gulf and Afghanistan Infectious Diseases Disability Benefits Questionnaire
21-0960M-5 Flatfoot (Pes Planus) Disability Benefits Questionnaire
21-0960M-12 Shoulder and Arm Conditions Disability Benefits Questionnaire
21-0960G-3 Intestinal Conditions (Other that Surgical or Infections) (Including Irritable Bowel Syndrome, Crohn's Disease, Ulcerative Colitis, and Diverticulitis) Disability Benefits Questionnaire
21-0960M-16 Wrist Conditions Disability Benefits Questionnaire
21-0960F-1 Scars/Disfigurement Disability Benefits Questionnaire
21-0960Q-1 Chronic Fatigue Syndrome Disability Benefits Questionnaire
21-0960F-2 Skin Diseases Disability Benefits Questionnaire
21-0960G-4 Intestinal Surgery (Bowel Resection, Colostomy, Ileostomy) Disability Benefits Questionnaire
21-0960K-1 Breast Conditions and Disorders Disability Benefits Questionnaire
21-0960N-3 Loss of Sense of Smell and/or Taste Disability Benefits Questionnaire
21-0960A-2 Artery and Vein Conditions (Vascular Diseases Including Varicose Veins) Disability Benefits Questionnaire
21-0960C-2 Amyotrophic Lateral Sclerosis (Lou Gehrig's Disease) Disability Benefits Questionnaire
21-0960J-4 Urinary Tract (Including Bladder and Urethra) Conditions (Excluding Male Reproductive System) Disability Benefits Questionnaire
21-0960H-1 Hernias (Including Abdominal, Inguinal and Femoral Hernias) Disability Benefits Questionnaire
21-0960I-3 Infectious Diseases (Other than HIV-Related Illness, Chronic Fatigue Syndrome, or Tuberculosis) Disability Benefits Questionnaire
21-0960M-7 Hand and Finger Conditions Disability Benefits Questionnaire
21-0960M-8 Hip and Thigh Conditions Disability Benefits Questionnaire
21-0960M-10 Muscle Injuries Disability Benefits Questionnaire

21-0960C-11 Seizure Disorders (Epilepsy) Disability Benefits Questionnaire

21-0960L-2 Sleep Apnea Disability Benefits Questionnaire

21-0960M-1 Amputations Disability Benefits Questionnaire

21-0960M-3 Non-Degenerative Arthritis (Including Inflammatory, Autoimmune, Crystalline and Infectious Arthritis) and Dysbaric Osteonecrosis Disability Benefits Questionnaire

21-0960G-7 Stomach and Duodenal Conditions (Not Including Gerd or Esophageal Disorders) Benefits Questionnaire

21-0960H-2 Rectum and Anus Conditions Including Hemorrhoids) Benefits Questionnaire

21-0960I-1 Persian Gulf and Afghanistan Infectious Diseases Disability Benefits Questionnaire

21-0960M-5 Flatfoot (Pes Planus) Disability Benefits Questionnaire

21-0960M-12 Shoulder and Arm Conditions Disability Benefits Questionnaire

21-0960G-3 Intestinal Conditions (Other than Surgical or Infections) (Including Irritable Bowel Syndrome, Crohn's Disease, Ulcerative Colitis, and Diverticulitis) Disability Benefits Questionnaire

21-0960M-16 Wrist Conditions Disability Benefits Questionnaire

21-0960F-1 Scars/Disfigurement Disability Benefits Questionnaire

21-0960Q-1 Chronic Fatigue Syndrome Disability Benefits Questionnaire

21-0960F-2 Skin Diseases Disability Benefits Questionnaire

Remember Our Veterans

Dedicated to America's Heroes - Our Veterans

Charles Fettes is a retired Master Chief Petty Officer (U.S. Navy) who has worked in veteran's service for the past nineteen years.

He retired as the office manager for the American Legion Veterans Affairs & Rehabilitation, Department of Michigan, in September 2010 and accepted the position of Citrus County Veterans Service Officer in December of 2010.

He is married to Barbara and resides in Homosassa, Florida.

38178947R00085

Made in the USA
Lexington, KY
30 December 2014